TIMES of WAR and PEACE

Dealing with Kids' Concerns

Dr. Susan Goldberg

art · Gail Geltner

Annick Press Ltd.

Annick Press Ltd.

Annick Press gratefully acknowledges the support of The Canada Council and the Ontario Arts Council.

Canadian Cataloguing in Publication Data

Goldberg, Susan
    Times of war and peace

ISBN 1-55037-202-5

1. Children and war. 2. War—Psychological aspects. 3. Fear in children. 4. Emotional problems of children. I. Title.

BF723.W3G65 1991   155.4   C91-094241-2

Distribution for Canada and the USA:
Firefly Books Ltd.,
250 Sparks Avenue
Willowdale, Ontario M2H 2S4

Printed and bound in Canada
by Friesen Printers

Table of Contents

Introduction

W hen the active war in the Persian Gulf came to an end, for many North Americans this also terminated concern about the effects of war on children. For others, war in the Gulf was only a reminder that conflicts within and between nations are ever present in our time and that the potential for global conflict remains. The termination of one conflict is only a temporary respite and the need to help children understand war and develop peacemaking skills continues. For those working in peace education, the development of positive and constructive responses to conflict is viewed as a long-term constructive alternative to war. This book is intended for educators, parents, community workers and all others who share this viewpoint.

It is significant to note that the course of history has brought war increasingly closer to civilians. It has been estimated that in the First World War, only 5 per cent of the casualties were civilians; in the Second World War, the corresponding figure was 50 per cent. By the time of the war in Vietnam, the figure had risen to 80 to 90 per cent and some estimates for recent wars in the Middle East put civilian casualties as high as 97 per cent. Thus, it is not surprising that there has been a documented increase in civilian worries about the possibility of war, among both adults and children, even in North America where direct involvement in war has been extremely limited and geographically distant.

Communication technology also brings distant events into our living-rooms on a daily basis. During the 1970s and 1980s a relatively small group of concerned activists began responding to these concerns by documenting children's awareness of the threat of global destruction.* The research accumulated during this period indicated that children were frightened by the threat of global war, that they gained most of their information from television and that they discussed these concerns only minimally at home or school. For the most part, adults had little response to children's fears and to the lack of information or dialogue. Many well-meaning parents, educators, and mental health professionals maintained that if peace activists would only stop asking questions, young people wouldn't be worried about nuclear weapons or war.

This point of view had to be reconsidered, however, when in January 1991 war broke out in the Persian Gulf. This time North Americans were directly involved and the conflict was presented "live" on television while routine programming was pre-empted. Suddenly, parents, teachers and mental health professionals were alarmed at the continuous exposure of children to the horrors of war. In one children's hospital the psychiatric consultant found hundreds of child-patients were alone in their rooms watching "the war" while oblivious hospital staff pursued routine activities. Everyone wanted to know what to tell children, how to reassure them, and what could be "safely" discussed.

Times of War and Peace has been written as a response to this need. It is a resource for peace educators—peace education in its broadest sense, which includes knowledge and skills that can create a peaceful world. Thus, we focus on understanding the causes of war, such as racism and economic inequality, and on developing media literacy as well as the more traditional conflict resolution skills. Of course, the ideas and strategies presented here are only a start. The resources section is designed to help you find more books, films and videos as well as to put you in touch with organizations in your region.

*FACING THE NUCLEAR AGE: Parents and Children Together, copyright 1985 by Dr. Susan Goldberg. Published by Annick Press Ltd.

Impediments to Peace Education: Documenting Children's Concerns

A major impediment to the implementation of the ideas proposed here is the belief that they will induce unwarranted fears in children. Therefore, it is useful to review what has been learned about children's fears of war over the past 20 years of systematic research.

In the early 1980s, the popular press was filled with stories about the psychological impact of the threat of nuclear war on children. They emphasized the frequency with which children experienced this anxiety and suggested that social problems such as school dropout rates, adolescent pregnancy, and drug abuse could be attributed to the overwhelming psychological impact of the threat of global conflict on personality development. If this analysis is correct, it is hard to justify classroom discussion of this potentially psychologically damaging material. However, is there any evidence to support these strong claims?

The study of children's fears is not a new endeavor: it began in the 1930s. Early surveys (up to and through the 1950s) rarely reported war among children's fears. However, by the mid 1960s it was among the most prevalent items mentioned. For example, Sybille Escalona, a child psychiatrist, surveyed 350 children between the ages of four and adolescence and asked "How do you think the world might be different 10 years from now?" Although she did not mention war, 70% of the children surveyed mentioned "the bomb," "nuclear war" or

7

described a destroyed world. Some of these early studies were conducted by having researchers describe threatening situations and asking youngsters how they would feel if this happened to them. Such surveys may, in fact, have created the phenomenon they wanted to study. However, surveys of this type continued through the '70s and were effective in demonstrating that children did worry about global destruction.

In the early 1980s, efforts to study children's concerns about war became an international effort and studies were conducted in Europe, Australia and the Soviet Union as well as Canada and the U.S.A. These studies were designed to a) compare fears about war to the future-oriented worries of youngsters; b) assess the effect of worries about war on other ideas and attitudes, and examine the impact of various sources of information. Around the world the importance of children's worries about war were evident. When students were asked "What are the three things that worry you the most?" or "When you think about the future, what are the three things that worry you most?" worries about war were the most common item mentioned.

However, one Canadian study indicated that the frequency with which such worries occurred did not exceed that of worries about national unemployment or personal job/career plans. Those students who reported worrying about nuclear war most frequently also spent more time thinking about their personal career plans and were most likely to say that they and others could do something to prevent nuclear war.

The "worriers" were also more likely to discuss concerns about nuclear war with others (at home, school, or with friends). Thus, these data suggested that the "worriers" were also the informed and optimistic and indeed, among those who said they never worried about nuclear war (including some of those who mentioned it as one of their three greatest worries) most reported that there was nothing they, others, or their nation could do to prevent global war. These data for the first time suggested that worry about war or nuclear war can be empowering rather than psychologically damaging; that worry and talking with others can be a constructive response to an issue that is realistically worrisome.

Surveys from around the world were effective in destroying several myths about children's worries about war:

1. *That children only worry about war if their parents are peace activists.* A Canadian study documented that though only 10% of students said their parents had "done something" to prevent nuclear war, over 50% mentioned war as one of their three main worries about the future.

2. *That only middle class children (i.e. those who have nothing else to worry about) worry about war.* Among the surveys that have been done, there is no evidence to support this point of view. In most

> Surveys from around the world were effective in destroying several myths about children's worries about war.

cases, social class has not been related to the degree of worry expressed by children. However, some of those which did report such an association found that working class children worry more.

3. *If adults don't raise the issue, children won't worry about it.* In a series of grade school interviews in an inner city school in Toronto, where no mention of war or peace was made, 20% of second graders, 50% of fourth graders, and 80% of sixth graders spontaneously mentioned war as a concern.

4. *Peace education in school would be children's main source of information about war.* When asked to rank their main sources of information, the majority of students surveyed listed television first, followed by other media sources. Surveys repeatedly show that television is children's primary source of information. Yet we know that the approach of the television industry to global issues is not designed for the child, nor is it intended to be

educational. In educational needs surveys done in California and British Columbia a majority of students in grade five and up indicated they had learned little or nothing about current global conflicts in school.

These studies outline a different picture, one that is good news for peace educators: worry need not be emotionally damaging. Systematic teaching about global problems is desired by students and contributes to optimism and empowerment.

Response to Children's Concerns: What Can We Do?

D uring the 1980s when children's war fears were just beginning to be discussed, I ran numerous workshops on how to effectively respond to them. The workshops used a very simple format. Each participant introduced him/herself and shared experiences in which children had raised issues about war or weapons. Then we listened very carefully and recorded (audio or video) conversations with children on the topic, with a focus on what children really wanted or needed from adults in these situations. A discussion then followed in which we developed strategies and ideas for meeting those needs. One very striking phenomenon was that the same themes emerged in almost every session. It was only after several years of conducting such workshops that I also realized that the advice we were constructing was no different from recommendations about discussing any sensitive issue with children: listen, be honest, engage children constructively, and provide appropriate models in our own behaviour. The guidelines below represent an adaptation of these ideas developed for the Toronto Board of Education in 1991, shortly after the war in the Persian Gulf broke out.

Talking About Global Conflict with Children

On virtually any night of the week children are able to witness conflict taking place somewhere on the globe. Even a cursory glance at a newspaper, the television or a magazine shows some level of strife ranging from out-and-out armed combat to threats of military intervention to civil war. Examples are found all over the globe.

All this means that it is undeniable that conflict is very much on the minds of children. How can we best respond to children's concerns? The following are some suggestions. These are general ideas which can be adapted for any age group or context.

Talking about war with children is similar to talking with children about other sensitive issues (e.g. sexuality, racism, etc.). If you have had the experience of talking with children about other emotionally sensitive issues, think back to these experiences and draw on them.

Taking care of ourselves

What makes these issues so difficult is that we as adults find our own emotions in turmoil. We have our own fears and anxieties. It is important not to let these get in the way of listening to children or to "take over" the home or classroom. We need to

fulfill our own needs by making connections with other adults. Informal discussions with close friends, teacher or parent study or support groups, etc. can fill this need.

Listening

It is important the youngsters have an opportunity to express their concerns and to feel that adults are taking those concerns seriously. It is natural to be upset by children's worries about global issues and to want to make them go away. False reassurance, however ("Don't worry"), is generally not helpful. It is helpful to let children know they can share their concerns and not be alone when they are fearful.

Facilitating discussion

There will naturally be differences of opinion about specific events. Emphasize that each individual is entitled to his/her own feelings and opinion. In group discussions, try to find common ground (e.g., we are all upset, angry, frightened, even though we disagree on solutions). It is helpful to model how to express opinions of your own while respecting other opinions ("I understand that Mary feels . . . She has a good point. However, I think . . . "). You may use the opportunity to talk about handling differences of opinion in the classroom or among friends as a small scale model of international disagreements. Help children to distinguish between the idea and the person, between individuals and governments.

Honesty

Share your own concerns in an honest way. It is worrying to youngsters when adults admit fear BUT it is more worrisome to feel that adults are too scared to talk or are hiding something. Youngsters may look to you as an authority for reassuring information: is the war going to come here? An honest answer might be "I hope not." Feel free to acknowledge your limitations while being willing to search for information: "I don't know. How could we find out?"

Reassurance

There are things about which children can be reassured. One young child thought the "gulf war" was taking place on the golf course behind her home. In this example, simple and straight-forward information can be reassuring. Children can also be reassured by information about peacekeeping and peacemaking efforts and by the knowledge that the adults in their lives will do everything possible to protect them in times of crisis.

Engaging children

Many children are upset and angry that adults have allowed this war to happen. It is helpful to channel these feelings into constructive activities. For example:

1. Children can write to political leaders (local, national, or international) and to newspapers to express their views.

2. Children can be encouraged to express these feelings in art, songs, or poetry so that they can be publicly acknowledged.

3. Children can begin to systematically gather information

that will help them understand the issues.

4. Children can participate in humanitarian efforts to aid victims of war.

In these times we all need to feel that we are not helpless; that we can do something. Discussion about constructive things that individuals and groups are doing can provide inspiration.

(Adapted from guidelines prepared for the Toronto Board of Education January, 1991.)

Adults as Models: Engaging Ourselves

Children may listen to what we say, but they also notice what we do, how we conduct our lives and the consistency between our words and our deeds. We are models for our children, and if we can respond positively to global issues, our confidence will reassure our children. Where is that confidence to come from?

Most adults who spend a great deal of time with children, whether as parents, teachers, or friendly companions implicitly know a great deal about how to respond to children's interests and concerns on many levels. It is when children raise concerns that touch our own strong emotions that this knowledge becomes inaccessible, overwhelmed by our feelings of distress and helplessness. It is by coming to terms with our own feelings, by empowering ourselves that we can truly help children. It is clear, then, that we as adults must be actively engaged in the issues of our time and develop our own political analysis in connection with other adults.

In most communities there are groups active in a variety of issues at various levels from very local to national and international. In the resource section we have tried to list some organizations that may be helpful, but it is impossible to provide an exhaustive list. You may also find it desirable or necessary to initiate a group of your own.

Knowledge as Power: Crisis as Opportunity

W hen war broke out in the Persian Gulf I was suddenly in demand to give advice about what to say to children. I was feeling angry, confused, and helpless about the war and I found myself automatically turning to the advice I had been giving to others for several years about talking to children about war and peace. I still thought it was good advice, but the crisis of the war somehow made it feel hollow and empty. One of the most challenging moments came for me when I facilitated a meeting of teachers from the Toronto schools and found myself facing over 300 emotionally aroused grownups wanting to vent their own frustration and rage  and consequently not really ready to take on the issue in their classrooms.

One teacher who spoke said he didn't feel that he could discuss the war in his classroom because he had Arab children and he thought they might be upset by the discussion. I replied that I hoped the presence of children of any particular group would not be the basis for talking or not talking about the war, that if the teacher could establish an accepting context and help children separate people from ideas, this was an opportunity for the children to hear a variety of perspectives and perhaps understand a different point of view from their own.

The teacher reiterated his concern and I then saw and acknowledged that the issue was not the presence or absence of any particular group in the classroom but the teacher's discomfort with the issues, particularly with addressing racism in the classroom. The moment passed and the discussion moved on, but I found myself returning to it mentally over and over because it marked my realization that in the tumult of this crisis we also had opportunities for direct learning experiences in several domains essential to peace education:

1. combatting racism
2. media literacy
3. understanding the economic causes of war
4. development of peacemaking skills (conflict resolution).

It is also the case that ongoing education in these domains will provide students with the basis for constructive and creative responses to crises when they arise. In the remainder of this section we provide examples of educators working in each of the above domains. Some of the examples represent long-term ongoing programs while others illustrate responses to particular events.

The Economic Basis of War

Often when war breaks out, the discussion in the media, in the home, and in the classroom focuses upon relatively immediate causes: the aggressive action of one nation toward another, confrontations of different groups within a country. Sometimes an immediate economic issue is evident. During the war in the Persian Gulf, access and control of the important resource of oil was often mentioned. However, the understanding of a long history of economic deprivation or exploitation is rarely available to adults and certainly not comprehended by children.

North America is increasingly encountering refugees from war-torn countries who can testify to the vast discrepancy in standards of living. Yet few North American adults, and fewer children, comprehend the extent to which their relatively privileged life, maintained in part at the expense of people in poorer countries, can promote the conditions for war.

One way of sensitizing children to this issue is through a game simulation in which they find themselves deprived of something desirable while a few "privileged" peers have an embarrassment of riches. An example of one such game suitable for grade school children is outlined below.

"Treat, treat... who gets the treat?"

A development education game for children.

This game is adapted from one originally prepared by Global Community Centre in Kitchener, Ontario.

PURPOSE: — To give children an experience of having little control over their ability to meet their basic need for food and resources.
  — To allow children to talk about the feelings that even simulated "deprivation" causes, and to increase their empathy with people who know suffering as a daily event.

(Optional: To provide an experiential base for a discussion of the development-related roots of war.)

AGE GROUP: Best for children between grades 5 and 8. Has been used successfully with good readers in grade 4 and could easily be used in high school.

19

SUPPLIES: Peanuts, bowl, a set of "chance" cards for each group playing. (See pages 21 to 27. Photocopy and cut out the cards.)

DIRECTIONS:

If the group is very large, divide it into sub-groups of no more than 20. Place a bowl of peanuts and a set of chance cards on the table and ask all the children to gather around. (Cards should be stacked in order with #1 on top.)

Explain that each person will take a card in turn, read it aloud to the rest of the group, and take as many treats from the bowl as the card says.

Have the children keep their cards until the discussion session.

IMPORTANT: Be sure there are enough cards to give each child an even number of turns. For instance, in a group of 12 children, you would have to remove card number 37 to allow each person to have three turns.

QUESTIONS FOR DISCUSSION:

1/   Have the children tally the number of treats they received. Chart those numbers on a piece of newsprint for them. Generally, the percentages work out to the exact percentages of people who are overfed in our world, adequately fed, underfed, and starving.

2/   Ask the have-nots in your group what they felt like when they saw some of the children getting large amounts of treats and eating them quickly. What did they feel like doing at that point?

3/   Ask the haves what they felt like and what these angry feelings made them want to do.

4/   Point out that the bowl of peanuts actually contained enough for all. Invite the participants to devise a fair system for dividing the remaining peanuts. (Don't be surprised if the have-nots quickly give up the polite discussion and begin grabbing for peanuts. This game often ends with a mini-free-for-all in which everyone grabs one handful and the person acting as arbitrator—the UN or a government—gives up on a negotiated resolution. It is also common for children to spill some of the peanuts in the tussle—a good opportunity for the teacher to raise questions about whether those resources were well-used when people had to resort to "war" to get a share.)

5/ Ask the children if they would be willing to play this game again. Would they play it again if they were really drawing lots for their own food supply for a day? What about for a week? Why or why not?

6/ Ask the children what they would like to do to put their new insights to work? (One group decided to collect money for the World Development, Service, and Relief Fund. Another group invited their representatives in government to come to their church to discuss development and peace and what he was doing to solve the development problems of poor countries and therefore to prevent more wars from breaking out.)

PEANUT GAME CHANCE CARDS

1. A flood wiped out your family's crops and you have no money.

Take NO treat.

2. Because of the efforts of a Canadian well-driller, your village has water to use on the fields for the first time.

Therefore you can now afford ONE treat.

3. You have just graduated from school and were lucky enough to get a job. However you need all your money to help send your younger brother to school.

Take NO treat.

6. Your father got free schooling and now has a very good job.

Take 10 treats and eat as many as you can as fast as you can.

4. There was such a bad drought that the crops your family planted didn't grow.

You CANNOT have a treat.

7. Your parents formed a co-operative farm with 4 other families. For the first time they had a large enough crop to sell a little extra in the nearby town.

You can now afford ONE treat.

5. Your family's small farm produced very little this year because you could not afford fertilizer costs. The oil companies and fertilizer companies from America made record profits.

Take NO treat.

8. Your family's crop was mostly eaten by locusts this year. You did not treat it with pesticide because the company would not give you credit until your crop was sold.

Take NO treat.

9. Your parents both developed black lung from working in the coal mines since they were 10 years old. Now they are too ill to work.

Take NO treat.

12. A volunteer worked in your village last spring, demonstrating simple ways to improve their nutrition. Your family now keeps a few chickens to provide eggs— you eat much more protein now than you used to eat.

You can now afford ONE treat.

10. Your family grows coffee. Since the crop was very good this year, there is a surplus and the coffee buyers from the northern countries refuse to pay the price they paid last year.

You may have only ONE treat instead of the two you got last year.

13. Your brother receives a scholarship to attend school in Canada. Everyone is happy for him, but it means you will have one less person in the sugar-cane harvest this year.

Take 1 treat instead of the 2 you took last year.

11. Your father's union has just won a big wage increase and a cost-of-living clause in their contract.

You may take 8 treats. Eat as many as you can as quickly as you can.

14. Your father is blind due to an infection in the water. Your mother cannot work because she has no one to look after the children.

Take NO treat.

15. Your family has just harvested a big crop of jute (used to make burlap bags). Since many of the companies that buy jute have been bought out by plastics companies, there is no one to make jute bags any more and the price for your crop has fallen.

You may have only ONE treat instead of the two you got last year.

18. Even though your parents are both unemployed, they get insurance payments.

You may have 4 treats. Eat as many of them as you can as quickly as you can.

16. Your family owns and runs a small business. Your government made special programs available for you, and everyone has been able to work hard all year.

You may have 8 treats. Eat as many as you can as quickly as you can.

19. Your father has worked for the last 6 years at the shoe company in your town. Nearly everyone works there, but now the company has begun to lay off the workers. It says it is cheaper to make the shoes somewhere else and import them for the people of your country.

Take NO treat.

17. Your father cannot get a job because he cannot read or write. (There was no school in your village when he was young.)

Take NO treat.

20. You have harvested a big crop this year. You would be able to afford 3 treats if the farm were yours. But a rich man who lives 100 km away owns the land and takes 2/3 of your income as rent.

Take ONE treat.

21. Your father has just lost his job in a factory that makes cloth. The wealthy country which had been buying much of this cloth decided it should produce its own cloth.

Take NO treat.

24. Your family has just inherited a great deal of money from a wealthy relative.

Take 12 treats and eat as many as you can as quickly as you can.

22. Your family's food bills have gone up 50% this year because the rich people around the world have been eating a great deal more beef. That meant they needed the grains and soya beans you usually ate, to feed their cattle.

Take TWO treats, but eat only one. At the end of the game, give your second treat to the person who got the most.

25. Although your family is one of the wealthiest in your village, they have just spent a lot of money for your grandfather's funeral. (People would have thought that you were very disrespectful if they hadn't.)

Take only ONE treat.

23. Your father has a good job, but he has to spend all of the income on school fees for you and your three sisters because you are black. White children in your country get free schooling.

Take only ONE treat.

26. All of your family's income this year was needed to cover the hospital bills when you had a broken leg. There is no insurance.

Take NO treat.

27. Your father works on a fishing boat, but the fish he catches are sold to feed the pets of wealthy people.

Take TWO treats, but eat only one. At the end of the game, give your second treat to the person who got the most.

30. Ever since the pesticide company from another country built a plant in your town, people have been getting strange illnesses. Now your father has become so ill that he cannot work. Some people want the plant to leave, but there are no other jobs.

Take NO treat.

28. Your father works at an iron mine. He and the other miners have been asking the company to raise their wages, which no longer cover the costs of bare necessities. The company says it will not because it would cut its profits—in fact, it will move away if the miners don't keep quiet.

Take only ONE treat.

31. You have just helped the family harvest the crop of cocoa beans. It was hard work, but you all worked together. Too bad it took you out of school.

You can afford ONE treat.

29. Your parents both work because your community has a bus for transportation and a school to keep the children during the work day. Their wages are not high, but you are better off than many.

Take SIX treats. Eat as many as you can as quickly as you can.

32. Your family had a good harvest this year but just as you were about to sell it to the grain company, someone discovered oil on the land where you farmed. The government sent the army to chase you away; they burned your grain. Now you are a refugee.

Take NO treats.

33. Your older brother has found a job in a fancy hotel, working as a porter for tourists who come from Europe and the U.S.A. and Canada.

You can afford ONE treat.

36. Your family won the lottery this year. You got a medium-sized prize.

You may take TWO treats.

34. Your mother and father were kidnapped by the secret police. You and your sisters have lived with your grandmother until now, but she has just died. Now you will have to shine shoes on the streets; your sister will become a worker in a factory making computer parts.

You can afford ONE treat.

37. Your father is the president of a company mining bauxite in Brazil.

Take 8 treats and eat them quickly.

35. Your father left your mother and the children. Your mother worked for a while, but she missed so much work when your little sister became ill that she was fired. Now you live on welfare.

Take NO treat.

38. Your family lives on an Indian reserve. Your grandfather was a hunter, but now there are laws that forbid hunting in your area. There are no jobs and no place to go. Your family has to live on welfare.

Take NO treat.

Combatting racism: Facing History and Ourselves

Facing History and Ourselves is an organization that has developed programs to deal with the issues of racism, prejudice, and oppression. It uses the history of the Holocaust as a case study in which students examine issues such as the abuse of power, unquestioning obedience to authority and the ways in which abuse was resisted. Students are encouraged to seek the connections between history and their current concerns and choices, to consider how racism, anti-Semitism and violence affect their lives, and to consider how they would have acted if they had been participants in the events of World War II.

(For more information about the Facing History Foundation and the resources it provides, see pages 36 to 38 and the organization list in the resources section.)

Here are stories from two teachers' experiences in this program and the effect their work had in empowering students.

The Challenges of Teaching in a Multicultural Environment

by Jaime Wurzel

In an article in Facing History and Ourselves News several years ago, Professor Wurzel examined the teaching of reflective thinking through Facing History in multicultural classrooms. Here, he considers the kind of open and introspective analysis which teachers and curriculum developers in a multicultural environment must provoke from the content they teach if it is to truly engage students within a classroom and school community.

It was the beginning of spring. Children played in the school yard waiting for the bell to ring and the routine to continue. The sections of worn-out brick, sloppily covered with tar, were almost hidden by the radiant noon sun. The large, turn-of-the-century building stood surrounded by urban decay, but was filled with the loud voices of adolescents and their silent hopes.

I was struck by the cultural diversity present in the yard. In one section played Hispanic children. I recognized some of the girls. Flor's large dark eyes carefully inspected my tape recorder case. "Are you going to talk to me again today?" she asked in Spanish.

"No, I already interviewed you. I need to talk to some other classmates." She was disappointed.

Nearby a group of African-American boys sat on the stairs leading to the main gate. They stared from a short distance at a group of four African-American girls jumping rope. They played while being bashfully aware that they were being watched.

Not far from them a small group of Cambodian girls stood

close to one another in a corner avoiding being stepped on by running active boys. Compared to the rest, their voices were whispers. There were also groups of white children playing with other white kids. In the world of this school, they were the minority.

I was delightfully aware of the diversity in the playground. I was equally amazed at the actual separation between ethnic groups. They seemed to be together but at the same time separate from each other.

I had been coming regularly to visit a seventh grade social studies class. The class, like the playground, was a colorful mosaic made up of people representing every part of the globe. I wanted to know, however, the extent and depth of the integration. I wanted to find out the impressions that the different cultural groups had of each other. Was this classroom a learning community? Was integration just being in a class together? After being together for almost a full school year, did they know anything about each other's cultures? Do they understand the similarities between them?

In groups, or sometimes individually, I took the children to a section of the library where we were allowed to talk. I had already talked to Flor and her girlfriends. I talked to Sampan, a Cambodian boy. I had also spoken separately to Darrel and Charlene, both African-Americans. I was increasingly aware of how much they all had to offer. They had some cultural information to share.

I found out that no one in the class, including the teacher, had ever mentioned the Cambodian genocide which had brought Sampan to this United States classroom. I learned that the African-Americans in the class did not know much about "the Spanish kids." I learned that the Hispanic girls sought always to be with each other. From what I observed and heard, I learned that everybody though of each other in terms of "them," never in terms of "us."

Recess was over. I waited for my group in the library. It was my time to talk to the Hispanic boys in the class. I expected Francisco, Walter and Luis. Luis came by himself. "I wanted to come alone. I did not want to come with them. They are going to come later."

"Why?" I asked. He shrugged his shoulders.

"Shall we speak English or Spanish?"

"English, I don't like Spanish."

"Where are you from?"

"I am American."

As we went on, it became clear that Luis, in spite of his name, in spite of his being labelled a Hispanic by the school, did not like to be considered as such. The tense demeanor showing on his Boricuan Indian face told me that he was not comfortable with his identity. "Who are your friends in this classroom?" I asked.

"I ain't got no friends in this class."

Walter and Francisco came in after Luis left. Walter and Francisco seemed more comfortable with the fact that they were Hispanic. We spoke mostly in Spanish, although Walter seemed more comfortable speaking English. Francisco talked about the fact that he was the youngest of twelve children. He spoke with pride about his father, the "Santero." His father had been the healer in their Puerto Rican village. Now he did the same in their neighbourhood. "Puerto Ricans came from all over to see him. He can cure many diseases." Walter, also Puerto Rican, nodded with approval. "Did you ever share this information with your class?" I asked Francisco.

"No, I never did. They would laugh at me."

Walter patiently waited to be the focus of the conversation. When I first met him I thought he was African-American. His physical appearance, the fact that his name was Walter, and that he seemed totally at ease with English reinforced this perception. As I began to know him, however, it became clear that he thought of himself as a Hispanic. But it was his perception of African-Americans, which he expressed during our conversation in the library, that left me shocked. I asked him to recount an experience with prejudice. Instead of a typical story of discrimination against Puerto Ricans, Walter told me more than I wanted to hear. "We moved from our neighborhood because of 'los morenos,' the Blacks. They kept their houses dirty. We did not want to be there. The Blacks once even attacked my mother." I stared at Walter in amazement. It seemed like he was not aware that he would be perceived as a Black young man himself. Walter went on. "Someday I am going to get a gun and I am going to get that morenos." Francisco was nodding in support. The bell rang. School was over for the day.

I went back into the classroom. The children had gone. The teacher was busy at her desk. I told her about my conversation with Walter. "We've got to do something about it."

"We can't. It is up to their parents," she answered. I did not pursue it further. She was busy preparing her next lesson on the Phoenicians.

On subsequent observations, as I sat in the back of the classroom, I watched the teacher proficiently deliver the facts and the students automatically record them in their notebooks. I watched Luis busy at his desk listening. I wondered what he was thinking about. I watched Flor secretly write a note to her girlfriend. I saw Walter put his head down on the desk, often ignoring the teacher's stares.

There was the teacher, who in a perfect tone of voice presented her well-organized lesson on Greek democracy. There were the occasional voices of children reading paragraphs from the text book, or the usual "me!, me!" sounds of adolescents enthusiastically wanting to be called upon. Yet, over all, I felt a heavy silence stemming from the fact that the conflicts behind the people in the class were never raised.

The routine of the classroom served the purpose of hiding the powerful issues which impact on the children's formation of their reality. Although what they learned was important from a traditional academic standpoints, its content did not have any bearings on how the children viewed themselves and how they viewed others. I could not help asking myself; what is the use of social studies curricula if it ignores notions of self-hate, inter-ethnic prejudice and violence? What is the purpose of schooling if it does not deal with the personal realities that the children bring to the classroom?

In another urban school, in another class, a group of black and white students sat facing each other ready to talk about racism. They had just finished watching a brief documentary film which depicted the process by which children were indoctrinated about the doctrines of the KKK. The film was shown as part of the Facing History and Ourselves unit of studies in a social studies classroom.

Waiting for an appropriate moment in the discussion, the teacher intervened to shift the focus from direct comments on the Klan to race relations in the school. "Haven't we made some progress? We are in a mixed ethnic and race classroom and we are talking about racism."

A Black student implied the opposite: "In school we behave differently toward each other, no one shows their real feelings, we just pretend to like each other. Outside school is a different thing." In-between other voices responding the comment, an African-American young woman agreed.

"I have white friends, they talk to me in school. But when I go their way, in their neighborhood, they are with their friends. They say nothing to me." She paused for a brief moment, then she raised her voice over the background of comments from her peers, "I want to know what's the difference between us, when I bleed red they bleed red!"

From the opposite side of the room another African-American

student responded in an even louder voice: "The difference is color!"

I stopped the video tape. I had been watching students from different backgrounds openly talk to each other about the realities of their own situations. In their comments, I sensed a balanced weaving of thought and emotion. The atmosphere of safety in the classroom allowed them to freely express their thoughts and feelings. The students were seeking to understand and resolve the conflicts they experience in their environment.

I could not help wishing for Walter to be in this classroom. I would have liked him to hear, "The difference is color!" Perhaps he would have begun the process of dealing with who he is.

Watching this Facing History video tape makes me realize that the existence of conflict is not the problem. In contemporary schools, conflict is inevitable. It only becomes a problem if we do not recognize its inevitability and if we do not learn to systematically deal with it in the classroom.

I watched the video tape of another Facing History classroom in another urban secondary school. The camera pointed to the word HOLOCAUST written in large capital letters on the blackboard. The students had just watched a film about the Nazi concentration camps. Since the program had been in effect for several weeks, the teacher and the students seemed comfortable with a discussion format on the topic of the Holocaust.

The conversation centered around the behavior of Nazis in concentration camps. There were those who talked about the psychological conditioning of Nazis to hate Jews and the nature of anti-semitism. Others justified Nazi behavior in relation to historical conditions in Germany between the wars; the humiliation of Versailles, and the need for collective self-esteem. Finally, someone who had been quiet all along broke the logical thread of the discussion and, somehow, narrowed the distance between intellect and emotion. "It is so easy to see the Holocaust as history that happened long ago in books. We are all capable of doing this, no matter who we are. It can happen to any of us. Human beings are . . ." Another voice interrupted in the background. "Yes, you can get so much power."

I stopped the tape. Again, I had seen powerful learning take place. Students made the connection between history and the human condition. They had, in the depersonalized environment of the school, brought out the theme of human vulnerability. Throughout the process of reflective discussion, they learned to disclose their humanity. They were coming one step closer to dealing with conflicts that exist within themselves and between cultural groups.

I could not help thinking about Luis, Francisco, Walter, and Flor. Facing History could help them validate their thoughts and their feelings. It could help them articulate in the classroom what they silently carry within themselves. If they were in one of these video taped classes, they could begin to reflect on the human condition; they could learn to understand human similarities. As they are linked in emotion and reflection with all their classmates, they could perhaps discuss openly the differences among them.

Dr. Jaime Wurzel is Professor of Multicultural Education in the Cultural Studies Department at Boston University and has recently published a book, "The Challenges of Teaching in a Multicultural Environment." Professor Wurzel uses the Facing History program in his methodology courses at Boston University.

A Toronto Teacher Reflects on Eight Years With FHAO

by Myrna Novogrodsky

In 1982 seven members on the staff of the alternative school in which I worked attended a Summer Institute in order to implement a pilot program based on Facing History for the Toronto Board of Education. The relationship between Toronto teachers and the Facing History staff grew over the years as more teachers attended Summer Institutes, as Facing History entered a partnership with the Toronto Jewish Congress to run an annual Canadian-based summer institute using local scholars, survivors and resources for Canadian teachers from all ten provinces.

Teacher training is interesting work, but after four years in a curriculum development job, I grew nostalgic for daily contact with adolescents and requested a two year leave of absence to re-enter the classroom. I was especially eager to teach the Facing History course again, both because the material had evoked such profound thinking and writing from my students, and

Facing History and Ourselves

"Facing History presents what is probably the most effective program educators have to deal with issues of racism, anti-semitism and other aspects of oppression and prejudice."

Recent history has revealed just how fragile the trappings of civilization are. In this century we have witnessed both the human capacity for monumental evil and indifference and the extraordinary capacity for care and compassion. In neighborhoods and nations, ordinary citizens have demonstrated how the ideals of democracy can be betrayed or realized by individual choice. Facing History encourages students to think clearly about human motivation, the nature of history, and the power of people to shape its course. The program deepens appreciation of each individual's action and generates greater respect for the dignity of human life.

What is Facing History?

Facing History is moral education. The target is hatred, prejudice, racism and indifference. The strategy is to reach young people with instruction in the history of the Nazi Holocaust and the Armenian Genocide as examples of what happens when morality breaks down. The plan is to reach our children's teachers who, with special training and innovative resources, can bring students through the understanding of terrible historical events to form the basis for maturity marked by the practice of good citizenship.

Since 1976, the program has reached nearly half a million students a year in educational settings with populations representing many social, economic, ethnic, and racial backgrounds. It has been successful in urban classrooms, rural schools, suburban communities, and in parochial, independent and public schools.

More than 30,000 educators, clergy, community leaders, parents and students testify to Facing History's impact as a compelling and profound educational experience.

"I came to this Institute with the idea that I would only be learning the history of the Holocaust. Instead I discovered a whole new way to approach everything I teach. It is imperative that students learn that they are part of a global community and become involved with that community's well-being."

Teacher, Chapel Hill, NC

What is Facing History about?

Facing History provides a unique approach to the study of the collapse of democracy and the rise of Nazi totalitarianism, examining such issues as abuse of power, unquestioning obedience to authority, and the ways in which such abuse was resisted. In workshops, seminars and in classrooms, teachers and students try to understand how neighbor turned against neighbor, and how indifference, denial and opportunism allowed the government to enact policies of mass murder. As students seek the connections this history has to their concerns and choices today, they are better able to consider how racism, antisemitism and violence affect their lives. Students think about the responsibility they have for protecting civil rights, and they examine the avenues available in a democratic society which enable them to make a difference in their own lives.

Facing History presents such difficult questions as:
How is an environment of mass conformity and racism created?
How does a nation move from protecting its minorities to defining them as the enemy?
Why did doctors, nurses and teachers, trained to care for human life, participate in the systematic dehumanization and murder of so many millions?
Why did lawyers trained to pursue justice participate in the systematic denial of the most basic human rights?
Why and how did some individuals defy the power of the state despite the dangers they incurred?
What are the consequences of avoidance, denial and distortion of history to society?

"Facing History is about more than just the Holocaust. It's about the reading and writing and the arithmetic of genocide. But it's also about such R's as rethinking, reflecting, and reasoning. It's about prejudice, discrimination, and scapegoating. But it's also about civic courage and justice. In an age of 'back to basics,' this curriculum declares that there is one thing more basic, more sacred, than any of the three R's; namely, the sanctity of human life."
A School Administrator

"In no other course was she (my daughter) exposed to real dilemmas as complex and challenging. In no other course has she been inspired to use the whole of her spiritual, moral and intellectual resources to solve a problem. In no other course has she been so sure that the risk mattered seriously for her development as a responsible person." A Parent

"Striking a balance between what to learn and ways to learn it is the hallmark of Facing History's approach to working with teachers. The secret, I believe, is not only in the selection of outstanding content but also in the orchestration of looking at new content and thinking about the teaching process." A Teacher

because many of my former students had reported that they had continued to think about the issues raised in the course for years to come.

Back in the classroom I found that although the rock groups students listened to had changed, that the colors for hair were now bright pink and purple, and that the faded jeans and tie-dyed shirts had been replaced by black leather with lots of heavy metal, the issues adolescents struggled with were still the same. Students were still engaged in meaningful discussions of obedience and resistance, activity and passivity, racism and discrimination.

The students I taught were in their final year of high school and I incorporated the Facing History material into an English course on the Literature of the Holocaust which was semestered and ran for five months. Students in the class were all working at an academic level; that is, they would qualify for university or community college admission if they chose post-secondary education. Many, however, had experienced unsettled adolescent years. Some lived on their own and worked part-time and studied part-time. Others had left school for one or two years and had recently returned. Two students had been active in the skinhead movement in Toronto. Ben was one of these students. As he proceeded through the course it was clear from his journal and from his comments in class that the Facing History curriculum was having a profound impact on his thinking and behavior.

Ben began to hang out with a group of skinheads when he was 14 years old. He was attracted to the music and dress, as well as to the skinhead attachment to nationalistic and patriotic ideas. He reports that the movement "gave me something to belong to." He was also deeply attracted to the fierce male peer bonding that was part of the movement. Ben felt the connection to the skinhead movement so deeply that he had SKIN tattooed to his shoulder blade, as well as EAST END BOYS (his group) tattooed on his forearm.

He enjoyed the clearly defined hierarchy in the skinhead movement. A good fighter, he won respect in the organization. He dropped out of high school and spent about two years "looking for action." It was only after a second, serious brush with the law when he was out on bail that he decided to return to school as an 18 year-old. He had been heavily involved in the skinhead movement for four years.

In his second year back at school he took the Facing History course. I asked Ben to talk about the ways in which the course changed his ideas. The first thing Ben began to question was his own extreme nationalism. He reports that he realized that his own "my country right or wrong" philosophy was exactly the same philosophy adhered to by many Germans, and it was this view that allowed the Nazi leadership to get people's cooperation in committing countless atrocities. Ben says, "I no longer accept all decisions of government as being right."

Toronto is a multi-racial, multi-cultural city in which over one half of our school's population comes from families in which neither English nor French is spoken at home. Ben began to question skinhead antipathy to foreigners. "Why shouldn't people hold on to their cultural identities? Why should all people dress the same? I no longer think that to be Canadian a person has to completely assimilate. In retrospect, I think that some of my former ideas were not only dangerous, they were wrong."

"I used to let things pass," said Ben. "Now I am more self-aware. I used to make a lot of racist jokes. Now they aren't so funny.

"The most difficult part of the course was looking at myself and realizing how easy it is for people to be manipulated to do the wrong thing. . .I don't want to go through life just being there. I want to do something."

Even though it is considered "wimping out" to leave the skinhead movement, Ben is clearly on his way out. His hair has grown in and his Doc Martin boots have been replaced by running shoes. He is currently working with an organization called *Justice for Children* which provides information to young offenders and advocates on their behalf. Although Ben was clearly questioning some aspects of skinhead philosophy before he took the course, he credits Facing History with changing his thinking and his behavior. "It should be compulsory for high school graduation," was his final comment.

Last month I ran into a former student at a social engagement. Gillian had been an outstanding student when I first taught

Facing History in 1982. She told me that she had kept her journal from the course and had recently re-read it. Now graduated from university, she realized that the course introduced her to issues that she continued to think about. Gillian agreed to meet me at my home and to tape record some of her reflections seven years after taking the course.

I opened the conversation by saying that Facing History looks at how people become victims, victimizers, bystanders and rescuers. I asked Gillian whether she had continued to think about these categories.

"Yes, I learned that I have been a bystander. It's easy to be a bystander—in cities especially. In my lifetime it is possible I will have to act in ways that will risk my life or my children's lives (if I have any). I know I may have to make critical and crucial decisions. . .I know now that we are all potential bystanders."

Recently I was traveling in India and to Indonesia. In Delhi we passed a man who was dying in the street. . .he looked like a Holocaust victim. I couldn't believe he was alive in that kind of

state. . .he was unconscious. We tried to talk to him and we gave him a little bit of money. We began to walk off, then we realized, what was he going to do with money? He couldn't move. We went back and he told us he was trying to get to a hospital across the busy street. We decided we had to do something about this. He had flies all over him—he was infected. . . We went across the street to the hospital to see if they would bring a stretcher and they wouldn't. . . We went back to where we were staying and we took our bedsheets and we carried him across to the hospital ourselves. In this case we did what we could do considering that we are not trained doctors. Also, he knew that we had done it. We had to decide how we were going to act and how we would feel if we did nothing. . . It was very much a symbolic thing because I don't know whether he survived. We went from being in despair to feeling empowerment because we did something.

That experience influenced me to change my life when I came home. Now I'm working for an environmental group doing public education.

That course made me aware of racial discrimination. The person I live with is from a visible minority and I am coming to a deeper understanding of how discrimination affects one's morale and sense of self.

Gillian and Ben are two students for whom the process of thinking about the issues raised in the Facing History course have made a difference not only in their private lives but also in how they are choosing to behave in the public sphere. I will teach the course again in the spring term. It will, as always, be both a challenge and a pleasure.

Myra Novogrodsky, Coordinator of Women and Labor Studies, Toronto Board of Education, is currently on leave and teaching in the City School, Toronto. She has been a member of the Facing History training team for the past three years.

Media literacy

Children (and adults) are constantly surrounded by the messages of television, radio, and print which have potent influences on our everyday life and on our ideas about global events. Often we are not even aware that the world depicted in the media is a constructed world rather than reality. During the war in the Persian Gulf, for example, many families were "glued" to their TV sets for long hours of "news". Yet no first hand accurate information was available. Reporters' activities were severely limited and the information was heavily controlled and censored by the U.S. government.

In times when war may not seem to involve us directly, many children spend long hours watching cartoons which promote commercially available toys that promote war as play. How can we encourage children to take a critical attitude toward what the media presents to them, whether "news" or entertainment?

Here are two examples of constructive responses to media images that encourage youngsters to think for themselves. The first article describes the activities of Pacijou, a Quebec group which initiated an effort to combat the promotion of commercial products that promote war as entertainment. In the second article, a high school teacher discusses how he handled his classroom activities during the Gulf War to encourage students to take a critical view of the news.

Pacijou and the War Toys Project in Quebec

by David Clandfield

The project kicked off in October 1987, with the publication of a colourful teachers' guide to an anti-war toy curriculum called *Cessez le feu!* ("Hold Your Fire!") It consisted of a series of activities designed to help students become aware that war is not a game; that their world of play and fantasy is increasingly being dominated by commercial products promoting violence and war as a form of play; and that there are better ways of settling differences than using fists or guns. The guide laid out activities designed for every age from pre-school children's activities in nurseries through the elementary, secondary and college years to adult education. It even included ways to include parents, since their collaboration would certainly be necessary if their choice of toys and presents was going to change.

Accompanying the curriculum proposal were the plans for a more concerted campaign with three principal focal points. In the elementary schools, children would be invited to give up the war toys they already owned to serve as the basis for a new public sculpture celebrating peace. Secondary students would engage in the development of an alternative form of publicity against the purchase and use of war toys and games. And while these two activities would be timed in the Fall of 1988 to influence Christmas season toy-buying patterns, the campaign would once again reach a climax at the annual Peace March of October 29, 1988.

Rather than approach issues of peace, nuclear disarmament and international cooperation through studying the intangible world of global politics, the curriculum guide's authors invite students to reach down into their very own culture to see how they are being conditioned to acccpt the inevitability and excitement of organized violence. The gestures they are asked to make emerge as a refusal of that intrusion into their own life; they are dealing symbolically with their own political

realities. Children are encouraged to take back their own play, their own leisure, their own culture. And once they have taken it back they can transform it into something different that will go out into the real world as proof that they made that gesture of refusal. That is the meaning of the peace sculpture made of war toys, and, to a lesser extent, the alternative advertising campaign designed to counteract the prevailing diet of commercials and advertisements peddling violence as a game.

Common Front Organizing

Pacijou did not sit back and wait for the campaign to develop its own momentum from the teachers' guide. By December 1987, they had engaged the interest of a number of broadly-based organizations in this campaign. A Colloquium organized by Pacijou in May 1988 brought together seventy-five representatives of various groups to plan the Fall's activities. So great was the mounting interest in it that by July they were presenting their ideas to delegates from 31 countries at the International Centre for Education in Human Rights and Peace in Geneva.

In September, the campaign began to roll in the schools. Twenty-five School Boards were now involved, mainly in and around Montreal and Quebec City. The campaign had the full support of all the teachers' unions in those areas as well as the principal labour federations (FTQ/QFL and CSN/CNTU). The Assembly of Catholic Bishops in Quebec dioceses had given it their approval and circulated statements to be read from the pulpits in support. Women's groups and international cooperation organizations were also on board. The Montreal transit authority allowed information tables to be set up in major subway stations. The City of Montreal endorsed the idea of a public monument to peace made of donated war toys. The National Film Board approved $250,000 for the making of a French-language film about the project, and now is preparing an English-language version soon to be released.

The Fall months saw a veritable media blitz on the French TV and radio. Pacijou members featured in 30 TV broadcasts; a hundred or so radio shows featured aspects of the campaign, not to mention the hundred or more articles in newspapers, weeklies and other journals and bulletins. A fifteen-part series on this theme was aired on Community TV, Channel 24.

And what of the results of the campaign? As the year came to an end, Pacijou could report that over 400 schools had participated in the curriculum campaign. 12,000 children had donated over 25,000 war toys of their own at an estimated value of over $50,000 to help build the peace sculpture.

A small number of secondary schools had run an anti-war toy publicity contest and the winning ads were so good that they were run in eleven magazines and on four radio stations throughout the province. There might well have been far more participation at the secondary level, but the campaign focussed principally on war toy collection in the elementary schools.

The march in Montreal drew 8,000 participants despite ferociously bad weather and featured parades of children bearing the war toys they had collected. A similar march in

Quebec City had lined up school buses for 6,000 children from the nineteen school boards of the region, but was cancelled because of the storm.

Since this time Pacijou has recorded and distributed a catchy popular song by a young man called Michel Landry: *La Guerre n'est pas un jeu;* the English version on the flip side of the cassette is called *Play for Peace*. A music video made from this song, dramatizing the message of the curriculum, has been remarkably successful. It ran in Famous Players cinemas throughout Quebec in the week before Christmas 1989.

And what of the peace sculpture? The latest news follows. The new mayor of Quebec City has endorsed the peace sculpture project and a site is about to the chosen from a list of five proposed. A huge financial campaign has been launched by school boards, unions and other groups in the region to pay for the sculpture. It is expected to be unveiled during the Peace March of October 1990. The City of Montreal has already chosen its site at the corner of Boulevard René Lévesque and St. Laurent, slap bang in the centre of the city, but further details are yet unknown.

Phase Two of the Pacijou project is now under way. It consists of two parts:

1. A petition was to be circulated by students for the removal of violent TV shows for children and for government funds to help produce quality nonviolent shows in their place. This is now complete as I write and 100,000 signatures have already been received by Pacijou, well in excess of the number first projected, and they are still expecting several tens of thousands more to come in from around the province in the next two weeks. Plans are now under way
   to form a delegation to present this petition to the Prime Minister, a delegation led by representatives of the major organizations that sponsored the petition: school boards, unions, Catholic Bishops, the City of Montreal, rural women's groups, psychologists, pediatricians, and Artists for Peace (represented by their president Antonine Maillet).

2. Organization of a cooperative contest among groups of schoolchildren to make alternative toys, games and stories that favor peace, human rights, international cooperation,

ecology and social justice. This project got under way in September 1989 and is scheduled to conclude in May 1990. The aim is to begin cooperative production of these toys, games and stories through Pacijou. This has led to the publication of Pacijou's second curriculum guide on August, 1989, *Imaginons des jeux, des jouets et des contes pour la paix ("Making up Games, Toys and Stories for Peace")*.

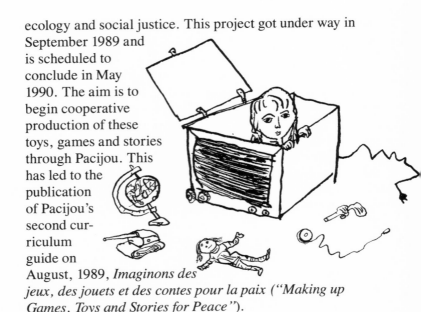

Transforming Children's Culture

The Pacijou project is nothing less than a cultural conversion plan. Whole school populations are to be mobilized to transform a children's culture based on violence and competition into one featuring values of peaceful cooperation. It seems utopian to consider this as a possibility in a world where that culture is increasingly dominated by multinational toy companies and the commercial products of Hollywood's giants.

I can't help feeling that such a project would be a stunning success even if it were implemented throughout one school board. And yet Pacijou are doing this throughout much of Quebec. It is real. It is happening.

Of course, it is too early to say whether we are seeing the first steps towards a greening of children's culture and the construction of a healthier society deep in the corporate-military heartland of North America. But the last time I was visiting La Maîtresse d'École, I saw a collection of the wartoys they were putting together as part of their protest. And one of the larger toy companies was on the phone in anguish to say that the huge robot shown on their box striding through explosions and laser rays was intended only as a construction toy. If the public relations people are getting worried, the campaign must be working. Who knows where it will all lead?

David Clandfield teaches French and Film at the University of Toronto.

*For further information, and full details of the Pacijou project, contact:
Pacijou Collective
c/o Diane Savid
3582 Rue Chambly
Montreal, Quebec H1W 3J9 Canada
Tel: (514) 523-7266

Fighting for the Truth:
The Gulf War and Our Students
by Bill Bigelow

Rethinking Schools asked Portland high school social studies teacher Bill Bigelow to write about ways to teach about the Gulf War. Even though the shooting war appears to be over, we believe that the issues raised by the conflict continue to be timely.

Teachers need to be instant experts. Whether the social explosion is in Nicaragua, South Africa, China or Panama, students have a right to expect that we will help them understand what's going on. As this school year began, Iraqi troops had occupied Kuwait and were confronted by a rapid build-up of U.S. forces in Saudi Arabia. Books on Iraq and Kuwait hadn't been tops on my reading list and, I confess, I was ill-prepared to be much of a resource.

Saddam Hussein would not win a popularity contest at Jefferson High School in Portland, where I teach. But students were divided about whether U.S. troops should forcibly expel his army from Kuwait or whether U.S. aircraft should bomb Iraq. In our class discussion circles, the only ground rule is that we remember we are a community of learners and everyone has a right to his or her opinion. Students raise their hands to speak, with whomever has just spoken calling on the next speaker. I interject occasional questions, but if I want to make a point I raise my hand and wait to be called on like anybody else.

These opinion-sharing sessions are a kind of research for me as I listen and take notes on how and why people feel the way they do, as well as for gaps in their understandings. For students, it's a time to express confusion, outrage, sadness or to convince others of the correctness of their positions. They learn a lot from listening to each other, but unless they get new information and analysis, these discussions become repetitive and tiresome.

Early on I relied too heavily on news articles and videos of nightly newscasts. It was a mistake as our discussions tended to mirror the shallow, ahistorical mainstream media reports. These rarely transcended descriptions of this bombing mission or that press conference and left us with none of the larger 'why' questions answered, or usually even asked. In contrast, I wanted to

encourage my students to constantly ask why, to seek out contradictions, look for the people behind the rhetoric and statistics, and not to begin from the assumption that our government is always right or that American lives are worth more than Arab lives.

This has been beg, borrow and steal time. I've never been more appreciative of being part of a community of creative and committed teachers. The following teaching ideas—some classroom-tested, some not; all incomplete and not an outline for an entire curriculum—are the result of drawing on this community.

The Arab "Enemy"

What comes to mind when students think of "Arabs"? Terrorists, rich sheiks, camel-riders? Where do our earliest lessons about Arabs come from? In our neighborhood video store, my co-teacher, Linda Christensen, located an extraordinary example of the stereotyping of Arabs—a cartoon titled "Popeye the Sailor Meets Ali Baba and the Forty Thieves."

In the cartoon, Popeye, a member of the U.S. Coast Guard, is dispatched to the Middle East where the cutthroat bandit, Abu Hassan, terrorizes towns and villages with his gang. Popeye is clean shaven, resourceful, and fearless. Abu Hassan is bearded, dark-skinned, burly; he rides through the desert with his band trailing behind, waving his saber and singing, "Now make no error, I'm called the terror of every village and town—Abu Hassan!" Plainly, he is evil—and stupid. All his men wear turbans and are indistinguishable, one from another. In cartoonland, Arabs speak a little English, but mostly gibberish.

When Abu Hassan raids the town where Popeye is staying (along with Olive Oyl and Wimpy) the townspeople offer no resistance and hide from the bandits. Popeye fights, loses this first encounter (Abu Hassan fights dirty) and Abu Hassan and crew steal everything not nailed down, including Olive Oyl.

Popeye trails the thieves to their hideaway and, upon seeing the wealth Abu Hassan has plundered, announces, "I have to give all these jewels back to the people." Meanwhile, Olive Oyl scrubs the clothes for Abu Hassan's turbanned look-alikes. Popeye confronts Abu Hassan, they fight, he eats his spinach, and to the martial melodies of John Philip Sousa, Popeye defeats the thieves. As promised, the Americans deliver the stolen loot back to the cheering townspeople. The end.

The cartoon portrays the Arab masses as helpless, uninteresting victims, terrorized by heartless thugs. The prognosis is grim, save for the presence of justice-loving, militarily potent Americans, in this case represented by Popeye. As they watched, my students listed how men's and women's roles were depicted and how Arabs were portrayed. Following the video, I asked them to write on what this cartoon might teach children. As always, students make connections that I miss. I'd noticed the lack of Arab women, but Kristina drew implications I hadn't considered:

The Arabs are portrayed as dirty, mean, thieves and murderers, stupid. Plus they all look alike, no originality. Those are the thieves, and then there's the peasants who are also portrayed as stupid, but they are also showed as cowardly and weak. The main thing I noticed is there's no Arab women in this cartoon, like the Arabs have no gentleness, or beauty, and that's very stereotypic.

Aashish:

Teaches children that sheiks from the Middle East are terrorists and USA is the best.

Michael:

Arabs are all the same people who wear headdresses and diapers; dark, shady, bald headed little bearded twerps who only use camels for cars, hide in vases, speak in an undesirable language and are spindly and have no musical talent. Most importantly, the U.S. has always been able to beat them down and we're in the right.

Portland teacher, Eddy Shuldman, showed the Popeye video twice to her students. The second time she asked them to imagine they were Arab children and to write about how the cartoons would make them feel.

Whether or not one is able to locate this cartoon, it would be valuable to find some media through which students might explore attitudes about Arabs and the Middle East and how these attitudes can lead us to certain understandings, or misunderstandings, about today's crisis.

I followed up with slides from a trip I'd taken to Jordan, the West Bank, and Gaza. It was a way of introducing students to the Palestine/Israeli struggle, but also erased the cartoon Arabs from students' minds and replaced them with real people: doctors, teachers, pharmacists, students, community organizers. We also read a short story by a young Palestinian-American student, Johara Baker, "A Day Among the People," which exposed students to the history and anguish of Palestinians in West Bank refugee camps. The goal was to give voice and persona to a people too often depicted as the inferior, inscrutable "Other."

Kuwait University professor Shafeeq Ghabra's "The Iraqi Occupation of Kuwait: An Eyewitness Account," *(Journal of Palestine Studies*, Winter 1991) could also be excerpted for use with students. Ghabra's is the best account I've seen to paint a human portrait of the degradation and brutality visited on Kuwaitis by the occupying Iraqi army. His account also chronicles the determination and creativity of the Kuwaiti resistance.

Exploring policy contradictions

Why is the United States involved in this war? An answer is beyond this article's scope, but one way to approach the question is to test official explanations against past U.S. conduct. Such a route might also lead students to a broader understanding of U.S. foreign policy.

At the date of this writing, February 25th, 1991, there have been numerous statements by President Bush, Secretary of State James Baker, and others about the objectives of U.S. involvement in the Middle East. Students remember most of these and we list them on the board. At first the mission was to protect Saudi Arabia from the alleged possibility of an Iraqi invasion. Soon, talk turned to the "liberation of Kuwait" and the "restoration of its legitimate government." Later objectives were to protect "our way of life," and American "jobs." Another oft-stated goal was to destroy Iraq's nuclear, chemical, and biological warfare capacities, in fact, obliterating its war-making abilities. More recently, President Bush spoke of creating a New World Order.

A constant refrain is that Saddam Hussein's invasion of Kuwait is intolerable because it violates the U.S. *principle* of support for national sovereignty—a principle underscored by numerous UN resolutions. To test U.S. commitment to this principle we should explore with students how the United States responded to other invasions and occupations.

Nicaragua: For fifty years the United States supported the Somoza family dictatorship in Nicaragua—"He's a sonofabitch, but he's *our* sonofabitch," FDR was reported to have said about Somoza. Decades later, during the U.S.-financed contra war against the Sandinista government, the United States had no use for the United Nations. In April 1984, Washington rejected World Court adjudication of U.S. disputes with Nicaragua, although the United States' refusal was a direct violation of the UN Charter. When the World Court ordered the United States to halt its aggression against Nicaragua in 1986, the Reagan

administration ignored the ruling. What accounts for the different response to Iraq's aggression?

Israel: During the last 15 years, the UN Security Council adopted 11 resolutions condemning Israeli aggression against Lebanon and other Arab countries. In August 1980, the Security

Council declared Israel's annexation of Jerusalem "null and void." In December 1981, the Security Council declared Israel's annexation of the Syrian Golan Heights "null and void." In December of 1982, a General Assembly resolution deploring Israel's invasion of Lebanon passed 143 to 2 (the U.S. and Israel). Earlier the General Assembly had condemned Israeli settlements in the Occupied Territories as "a serious obstruction to achieving. . .peace in the Middle East." Three Security Council resolutions demanded Israel's immediate withdrawal from Lebanon. The General Assembly has repeatedly criticized Israeli occupation of the West Bank and Gaza. A 1989 resolution was affirmed 151 to 3 (U.S., Israel, and Dominica).

One might ask *which* principle is upheld when Israel is rewarded with between $3 and $4 billion annually in U.S. aid while Iraq is hit with "smart" bombs and B-52s? [For high school students and our own background, recommend Norman Finkelstein's "Double Standards in the Gulf" in the November 1990 issue of *Z Magazine* (150 West Canton St., Boston, MA 02118). Middle and elementary teachers could also work with the information in the article.]

Namibia: UN Security Council Resolution, 435, passed in 1978, demanded UN-supervised elections in Namibia to choose a constituent assembly leading to an end to the illegal South

African occupation. For years, the U.S. government sat on its hands as Newmont Mining, Amax, Texaco, Standard Oil of California, and other U.S. companies exploited the colony's mineral wealth. Moreover, when South Africa invaded and occupied southern Angola in 1981, the United States vetoed a UN Security Council resolution condemning the invasion. Does U.S. intervention depend on the race of those whose rights have been violated? Perhaps the $2.5 billion U.S. corporations had invested in South Africa by the early 1980s factored into our non-response.

Rhodesia: In 1968, the UN Security Council approved mandatory economic sanctions against the racist white minority regime in then-Rhodesia, the first comprehensive sanctions ever imposed by the UN. Did the United States wait a few months for the sanctions to work and then propose military action? No. In 1971, the U.S. Congress called for the importation of Rhodesian chrome—joining Portugal and South Africa as the only countries officially violating the sanctions.

Iraq: Before his invasion of Kuwait, Saddam Hussein was, like Nicaragua's Somoza, our sonofabitch. As Hussein prosecuted a bloody war against Iran, the United States government provided him with military intelligence, aid, and favorable trade terms. Despite evidence his army used poisonous gas against the Kurds in the north of Iraq, the United States continued its aid. But after his invasion of Kuwait, with its close ties to the West, Saddam Hussein stopped being our pal. As the *New York Times'* Thomas Friedman recently remarked, in the eyes of U.S. policymakers, before the invasion, Saddam was "our thug and our bully . . . a bulwark against these wild, crazy, and uncontrolled Iranians."

Principles? What are they, when are they invoked and when are they ignored? These are vital questions to raise with students. Without doubt, Iraq's invasion of Kuwait was illegal and brutal. But because the United States has not responded with equal force and decisiveness to other illegal and brutal occupations, students need to probe more deeply to discover the source of our current intervention in the Gulf.

Who benefits?

A key question I raise with students as we walk—sometimes stumble—down the road to understanding U.S. intervention in the Middle East is: who stands to gain? Together, students and I brainstorm a list of beneficiaries from U.S. involvement in the Gulf.

Students know that maintaining control of "our" oil is a factor, but intuition tells them it must be more complicated. I think it is. In fact, the major export of Kuwait is not oil but money; money that's invested mostly in Great Britain and the United States. The major source of Kuwaiti income is interest on the money invested in the West—which, of course, ultimately does come from oil. The Kuwaiti elite has a direct stake in the Western economies. By contrast, Iraq made no such massive investments in the West and there was no assurance that it would use its new-found oil treasure to strengthen Western economies. Who stands to gain from the installation of Kuwait's former rulers? Certainly the Kuwaiti elite. But in a larger sense, it is the Western capitalists, seeking to re-establish the investment status quo from which they benefitted.

The peace movement likes to ask rhetorically, "What if Kuwait's major product were broccoli?" The implication is that, were this the case, U.S. troops surely would not have intervened. No? The U.S. government intervened by proxy in Nicaragua (major product: poverty, with a little coffee and cotton thrown in); conspired to overthrow the Guatemalan government in 1954 (major product: poverty and bananas); has poured $4.5 billion to prop up a repressive regime in El Salvador (major product: poverty, cotton and some coffee). The list goes on. These interventions appeared not to aim at control of a valuable resource, but at maintaining each country's compliance with the wishes of U.S. policy makers. Winner: those who benefit from existing power relationships.

In the Middle East, the elites of Saudi Arabia and the other emirates benefit from U.S. interventions as, at least for the moment, U.S. force ensures the stability of the Gulf oil monarchies. Ironically, despite the damage and terror caused by Iraqi Scud attacks, Israel also stands to gain from the war: the

Iraqi military threat is destroyed; international sympathy for the Palestinians wanes; war promotes increased divisions in the Arab world; the country rebuilds the underdog reputation tarnished by its suppression of the intifada and can lay claim to even more U.S. aid. In late February, for example, the U.S. approved 400 million in housing aid to Israel that had been stalled for several months.

The U.S. arms industry wins big. Peace is bad for business and the fall of the Berlin Wall sent shudders through the board rooms of military contractors. With half a million troops in the Persian Gulf, we no longer hear about a "peace dividend." As military industrialist Jim Roberts said recently to the cheers of his audience at the 5th annual Defence Contracting Workshop in Milwaukee, "Thank you, Saddam Hussein." The list can go on and students sometimes get carried away listing yellow ribbon manufacturers, flag sellers, political button dealers and other small-time war profiteers. The point is that from seeking beneficiaries of U.S. intervention our students can begin to make hypotheses about the source of that intervention. Students need to develop their capacities to make explanations in order for them not to settle for or be swayed by slogans. Arriving at the "right" answers—whatever those may be—is less important than engaging students in the process of probing beyond mere description.

Listening to media silences

I ask students where they get their news. We list the sources on the board: NBC, CBS, *The Oregonian, Newsweek*, etc. I point out that these entities are owned by huge corporations. NBC, for example is owned by General Electric, the tenth largest U.S. corporation and a major war contractor. [See Ben H. Bagdikian, *The Media Monopoly*, Beacon Press.] This raises important questions: What stories might these media be reluctant to pursue? What might they be unlikely to criticize? How does the quest for profit influence the character of a news show—say, Peter Jennings' "World News Tonight" on ABC (owned by Capital Cities, yearly after-tax profits in the $450 million neighborhood)?

Students can brainstorm on the topics they're *not* hearing about. For example, as late as two weeks after the U.S. began bombing Iraq and Kuwait, one of my students asked, "What's happening to the Palestinians in all this?" I too hadn't seen any network news story on the Palestinians, though I had heard a Pacifica Radio report that Gaza and the West Bank were under "curfew"—a sanitary description of round-the-clock house arrest with two-hour breaks every few days to buy food. A colleague is teaching at a university in Egypt this year, so I was also aware of the lack of coverage of the grassroots response in Egypt and other Arab countries to the allied bombing of Iraq and Kuwait.

In small groups, students might imagine themselves producers of a non-corporate sponsored news show: What do people need to know to make decisions about supporting or opposing the war? How should the anti-war movement be covered? (A recent survey by Fairness and Accuracy in Reporting, a media watchdog group, found that in the first five months of the crisis, the networks had devoted only 29 minutes of 2,855 total minutes of Gulf coverage to opposition to the U.S. military buildup.) What "silences" need to be filled in network coverage of Middle East events? Which questions are the media pursuing ("How many bombing stories were there today? What weapons systems have been employed in the ground war?") and which questions are they ignoring ("What principles *really* guide U.S. foreign policy? How is Kuwait tied to the world economy?") Students would need to ask themselves what is "news;" is it entertainment or education? If education, for what purpose? As alternatives to mainstream coverage, we might bring to class smaller circulation, non-corporate journals like *The Nation, In These Times, The Progressive, Z Magazine, The Guardian*, or *Middle East Report*.

The other evening, on Portland's local cable access channel, I watched a series of anti-war programs produced by the Gulf Crisis TV Project for Deep Dish TV [339 Lafayette St., New York, NY 10012 (212) 473-8933]. The shows gave me a new appreciation of the *pro*-war bias of the networks—how inherently limited is the media's obsession with *describing* the war rather than *explaining* it. Project reporters interviewed articulate critics like Palestinian scholar Edward Sid, MIT Professor of Linguistics Noam Chomsky, journalist Molly Ivins and anti-war activist Daniel Ellsberg, who were allowed to offer more than a one sentence quip. Each episode also featured anti-war demonstrations, with a broad range of tactics. Excerpts from these videos might prompt students to question the silences of the corporate media on key issues.

Students as journalists

When I teach the history of the Vietnam War, I play Lyndon Johnson and deliver a 1965 defense of U.S. involvement. Unlike President Johnson, in this role play I allow students-as-reporters to grill me in a press conference following the speech. For homework, students write an account of the speech and press conference as if they were reporters for different newspapers, ranging from conservative (a small town Oregon paper, the *Bend Bulletin*) to establishment *(The New York Times)* to left-liberal *(I.F. Stone's Weekly)* to radical *(The Guardian)*.

The goal is for students to see that news is "political." Which facts are included, how they are arranged, who is quoted and who is not, what broader questions are raised—consciously or not, a reporter's political perspective, and that of the journal for which he or she writes, determines the scope and slant of a story. As students listen to each other's very different news articles describing the same event, they experience this first-hand. Afterwards, we look at how each of these publications actually covered Johnson's speech.

The structure of this lesson could be adapted to today's events, with students questioning "George Bush," after a dramatic reading of, say, parts of his State of the Union address, then afterwards reflecting on and recording the results. Including a

"Saddam Hussein" in the press conference would point the lesson in a different direction, but could also be useful.

Doublespeak: The language of war

At a recent press briefing, Gen. Colin Powell, Chairman of the Joint Chiefs of Staff, said in reference to the Iraqi army in Kuwait, "First we're going to cut it off, then we're going to kill it." Another military press spokesperson said that Iraq was bombed so heavily because it was a "target rich" country. In press briefings, civilian casualties are referred to as "collateral damage." A characteristic of the language of the military and those who report on the military is that humanity is buried in a prose of lifelessness. Gen. Powell, for example, could have been talking about a rat or a cockroach. News anchors report "targets" being "hit" or "pounded" and "the enemy" attacked. The reality behind this antiseptic jargon is that human lives are being ended or altered forever—people aren't things.

The language itself can become a political force in shaping our and our students' understandings about the nature and conduct of the war. Edward Herman's "Double Speak" column in *Z Magazine* is a wonderful resource to provoke students to

critically read propaganda masquerading as news. Why, for example, is Iraq's invasion of Kuwait labeled "aggression" but the U.S. invasion of Panama dubbed "Operation Just Cause"? According to Herman's Doublespeak Glossary, the definition of "aggression" is, "moving armed forces into another country without our approval; also providing aid and comfort to an indigenous uprising of which we disapprove." Thus, by definition, under no circumstances can "we" ever be the "aggressors."

Have you noticed how many politicians, military spokesmen, and reporters call Iraq's invasion "naked" aggression? Herman comments, "Aggression is a bad business, but calling it naked aggression means we intend to do something about it. Our own aggressions, in Grenada, Panama, the Dominican Republic, and Indochina, were of course properly clothed in a cloud of justifying rhetoric." Why wasn't South Africa's invasion of Angola labeled "naked aggression?" Because we never had any intention of confronting the aggressor. We should ask our students: Why not?

English and social studies classes could pore over speeches, news conferences, and press releases reading for doublespeak. They could function as truth detectives ferreting out duplicitous or obscure statements and revising them with clarity and honesty as the criteria. Like Edward Herman, they could invent their own doublespeak glossaries. Or as they read they might talk back to and translate the writers' doublespeak, paragraph by paragraph.

In my classes at Jefferson, we practiced with George Bush's comment that he was going to kick Hussein's ass. "Kick ass." I said and write it on the board in big letters. "What exactly does that mean? When do you hear that expression?" Students suggested that kick ass might describe what a football or basketball team is going to do to its opponent or how badly a little boy is going to beat up another little boy. It implies a clear, unambiguous victory, winning—which took us into a discussion about what it would mean to "win" a war against Iraq: what then? We ended up with the possibility of a permanent U.S. force in Iraq, U.S. leaders in control of reconstructing Iraq's political system, increased internal conflict in countries like Egypt and Jordan, no resolution of the Palestinian question, etc. Kids saw that to "kick their ass" was a bit more complicated than Trailblazers 125, Lakers 99.

People behind the numbers

War is more than numbers; it's about people. Linda Christensen helped her students, through poetry, share their feelings and insights about the war's human consequences. She began with a letter she'd received from an ex-student.

. . . *There is this enormous hole that I can't explain— somewhere between my heart and my brain—I can't fill it with air-raids and tear gas . . .*

I don't know what to do with myself! I want to cry, to scream, to punch something!

I want to throw-up and get rid of everything. I can practically taste the bile on my lips—my stomach churns . . . and there is this enormous hole that even my children and the children after them will not be able to plug—it's been chiseled away for years . . .

I'm scared, Linda. Really scared.

Linda then shared students' poems about the Vietnam War and others from Vietnam veteran Yusef Komunyakaa's book, *Dien Cai Dau* ["You and I are Disappearing," "Prisoners" and "Thanks"]. Students wrote down and shared war images they'd found disturbing. These became the seeds of poems or letters the students wrote.

Dyan Watson's poem, "Gulf Games" is reminiscent of the football metaphor that is a motif running through *Hearts and Minds,* the outstanding film on the Vietnam War.

I don't remember when I received
  my first football
I can only see me and Dad
  in the backyard
  "throwing it around"
. . . (Dad) would run around in his old college uniform
  ducking here
  dashing there
  tackling invisible people
I always won of course—
  no matter what the score was
  When I made the school team
  Dad was always there
  cheering me on, praying for me
"Go son, go!"
Cheer for me now, Dad.
Pray for me.

For me, Dyan's poem is a human side of the little x's and o's that the parade of retired generals are so fond of manipulating as they chart the missiles, bombers, and tanks on the network news every evening.

Actions as antidote to cynicism

In Portland, there have been numerous high school and middle school student walkouts to protest the war. Students also joined the thousands of marchers in nightly protests after the bombing of Iraq began. Some of my students have also attended "pro-troop" rallies— many of which explicitly supported U.S. intervention. Whichever side students take, I encourage them not to be spectators, but to be history makers.

The more we use our classrooms to analyze war, oppression, and exploitation, the more important it is to allow—even encourage—our students to act. To keep students' passions and beliefs bottled up is to turn our classrooms into factories of cynicism and despair. Teachers may not be political organizers— it's not our place to recruit for our favorite activist groups—but students must come to view themselves as *agents* of change, not objects of change. Hope should be the subtext of every lesson we teach—especially now.

Bill Bigelow teaches at Jefferson High School in Portland, Oregon.

Portland teachers, working through the Curriculum Department of Portland Public Schools, have developed a curriculum guide to teach students about the Gulf War. For information, write: Bruce Richards, Curriculum Department, Portland Public Schools, P.O. Box 3107, Portland, OR 97227.

Conflict Resolution: DAS Peacemakers

Conflict can make everyday life painful for each of us unless we have some skills for coping with it. For most children, war is first understood by trying to relate it to everyday conflicts and the feelings that surround them. In recent years it has become clear that conflict which escalates to violence is a prominent feature in the home and school lives of far too many children. The first article below summarizes a review of bullying in Toronto schools and documents the seriousness of this problem. The second article tells us about how a conflict resolution program was first established in Toronto Downtown Alternative School (DAS). DAS Peacemakers originated in a primary school and was designed to provide children with skills for and experiences of resolving school conflicts. In 1991, DAS Peacemakers conducted demonstrations for other schools and parent/teacher groups. They have published some of their own peacemaking stories, prepared an audiotape of peace songs the children have written and are preparing a video about the program.

Bullying at School

by Suzanne Zeigler
and Merle Rosenstein-Manner

A t the request of the Toronto Board of Education, a study
was undertaken of the phenomenon of bullying among
elementary schoolchildren. The study has three components: a
review of literature on the topic; an exploration of what
schoolchildren of different ages know and understand about
bullying, using a story, discussion, and sometimes role-playing
to elicit this information in a whole-class context; and finally,
data on the incidence, correlates and frequency of bullying in a
random sample of Toronto elementary schools, using
questionnaires (based closely on those used in Scandinavia) to
collect information from students, staff and parents.

Bullying—the tendency for some children to frequently
oppress, harass, or intimidate other children, verbally,
physically or both—is familiar in many, perhaps most countries,
both in and out of school. Both familial and school factors
relating to bullying behaviour have been documented, and
studies indicate that such behaviour patterns may be long-term
and even inter-generational. In cities and countries where
attempts have been made to systematically document the
incidence and quality of bullying at school, a range of estimates
of frequency of bullying has been reported.

By far the most complete and systematic data comes from
Scandinavia, and particularly from Norway. The Scandinavian
data indicate that, among students roughly the same in age as
our elementary school population, about one in seven children is
bullied at school more than just once or twice in a term; and that
three percent of children experience bullying very frequently.
British and Irish studies, which are far less comprehensive than
the Scandinavian ones, suggest significantly higher rates;
between twenty and thirty percent in the first instance, and

about ten percent in the latter. An American study of children in Grades 3 to 5 also found that about ten percent of students were identified as seriously/frequently victimized. Bullying has been a major concern in Japan also.

In the Toronto study, which involved children in 22 classrooms in 17 schools, as well as a majority of all staff members, teaching and non-teaching, and several hundred parents in those schools, rates were found that were similar to the British and American ones, and higher than those for Scandinavia. According to our group data, collected in classrooms from Kindergarten up, bullying at school affects children personally from Grade 2 up. The individual questionnaires, filled out by students and their teachers and parents from

Grades 4 through 8, indicate that about one in five children in that grade range is victimized from time to time, and about one in twelve suffers from bullying, more than once or twice a term. There are significant gender and age correlates of bullying and victimization.

There are many existing interventions, some well field-tested, which have great promise for preventing bullying at school. Some of these, such as the Peacemaker program, are already in use at some of our schools, with reportedly successful results. The most ambitious and well-documented intervention was mounted in all Norwegian schools. Using print and audio-visual materials developed for the purpose, the program attempts to restructure the school environment to one characterized by a commitment and concern on the part of all members of the school community, regardless of age or role, to define bullying as unacceptable behaviour and to take personal responsibility for both preventing it and intervening if and when it occurs. This intervention is at the level of the whole school, and may represent a significant change in the operational definition of what is tolerated. At the two schools where the program was systematically evaluated, the incidence of bullying decreased by half.

---

from draft study on Bullying, Toronto Board of Education, January 1990

Children as Peacemakers Child Power!!

by Joey Noble

The following is based on the Peacemakers Project at Downtown Alternative School in Toronto.

In our militarized world, the ability to settle disputes peacefully is often thought of as a set of complex skills that only a few gifted diplomats possess. No wonder many adults would express skepticism about the ability of young children to solve their own conflicts. What we typically see (and what we *expect to see*) in a school play-

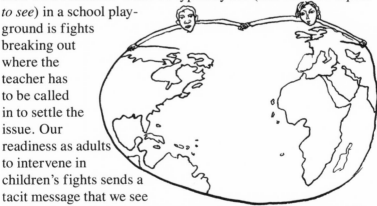

ground is fights breaking out where the teacher has to be called in to settle the issue. Our readiness as adults to intervene in children's fights sends a tacit message that we see them as basically incompetent to settle their own disputes. What lurks here is the idea that this whole business of conflict resolution is too difficult and sophisticated for mere children. Is this idea true, or are we simply in danger of making it true by the self-fulfilling nature of our assumptions about children's abilities?

I began to think about this issue when I first read *A Manual for Non-Violence and Children* (ed. by Stephanie Judson, New Society Publishers). Then at a Parents for Peace workshop, I had the chance to see a videotape about a programme in operation that makes the opposite assumption about conflict resolution: ie. kids can do it! The video was of the Conflict-Manager Programme initiated in 1982 in several San Francisco schools by Community Boards, Centre for Policy and Training, a non-profit foundation that specializes in spreading conflict resolution skills. Initially they had worked only with adults (e.g. on landlord-tenant or on customer-merchant disputes) but later they developed a programme for elementary school children that trained them in pairs to be able to intervene in playground fights and work out solutions without needing to call on a teacher. I was impressed with the video—the kids on the tape were actually able to solve their own problems. I couldn't help but notice that the children in the audience were completely captivated. The orange and black T-shirts worn by the conflict managers made them highly visible and attractive to the kids—a bit reminiscent of Ghost Busters.

We brought the video into my daughter's classroom, a combined grade 1-2-3 at Downtown Alternative School. After seeing it, several children spontaneously suggested: "Maybe we could do that here." So the children set in motion their own programme and chose their own name for it—Peacemakers.

Here is a thumbnail sketch of how the conflict resolution process works. If two children are fighting and can't solve it themselves they can choose to call in a pair of classmates (Peacemakers) to mediate a solution. The Peacemakers begin by asking the combatants a set of questions that gives the principled framework for reaching a solution:
• Do you agree to solve the problem? (Without commitment from both sides to stick with it the process can't work.)
• Do you agree to no interruptions?
• Do you agree to no name-calling?
• Do you agree to tell the truth?
The framework is deceptively simple for it is not all that easy to live up to, in practice, when people are feeling angry or hurt about what has happened. But both parties must agree to these rules before the process can move ahead. Then the peacemakers ask each child in turn, "What happened?" and each gets a turn to tell his or her side of the story. Sometimes recounting the

fight with others listening helps the combatants temper their anger and get a glimpse of the other person's point of view. After the story has been told the peacemakers ask each child, "Do you have a solution?" and again each gets a turn to answer. Sometimes the problem is worked out easily—the atmosphere of disciplined supportive listening and discussion does the trick and allows the two having the fight to come up with their own mutually agreeable solution. Other times the peacemakers' negotiating skills are needed to construct solutions that will be perceived as fair by both parties. The process often ends with a handshake aimed at sealing the agreement and healing the wounds.

When I interviewed the children recently about some of the problems they had encoun-

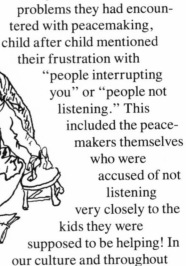

tered with peacemaking, child after child mentioned their frustration with "people interrupting you" or "people not listening." This included the peacemakers themselves who were accused of not listening very closely to the kids they were supposed to be helping! In our culture and throughout our schooling, it is speaking skills that are stressed and rewarded (eg. making speeches, scoring points in a debate), not the skills associated with careful listening. One of the strengths in the peacemaker programme is that it brings into focus the crucial importance of listening skills—conflict resolution strategies will not work without them. The children have even added a fifth rule to the ones that were given by the San Francisco project, a rule that reflects some of the very real, everyday frustrations:

• No plugging your ears. No running away.

It has been exciting to see how the children are elaborating on the initial rules as they are encountering some of the pitfalls with putting them into practice.

They have added a sixth rule:

• No touching people

This came about because sometimes when peacemakers put their hands on people, even just with the intention of separating them, the peacemakers themselves would end up embroiled in the physical fight. And there is another area of contention where a rule has not yet been formulated—what if one or both parties won't agree to solve the problem at the time (maybe because they are too angry or upset)? The children are debating whether it is okay to postpone peacemaking, and if so should there be a time frame on how long a fight can be left unresolved.

To be a peacemaker involves grappling with many difficult issues, including what to do when people lie to you or when they deny responsibility for their actions. It also involves gaining insights into some of the complex motives underlying fights, ie., digging for the truth. I was impressed to see how successfully the children resisted the temptation to use the peacemaker role to play judge and jury and take an open position on whose side of the fight, had the most merit. Rather, they understood the peacemaking role as one of mediating, of helping the combatants gain insight into each other's point of view, identifying misunderstandings, healing wounds, and even nitty gritty stuff like helping children save face when a fight is nearing resolution. The children expressed quite a deep appreciation of the importance of *not* siding with one party, but rather supporting both sides to work out their solution

* * *

The prevalence of Superhero play among young children has stirred up a lot of ambivalent feelings among peace-oriented parents and teachers. It is hard to stop it completely and we aren't even sure that we should be stopping it. Children undeniably have the developmental need to work out their feelings about power and control issues—especially in a society like ours which gives so little real-life opportunities to practice the use of power. The problem is not Superhero play itself, but the fact that the whole terrain has been occupied by the toy companies and their T.V. shows. They saturate the wavelengths with their monolithic militaristic message about power. For G.I. Joe, He-Man and Rambo, power equals domination *over* others (usually by physical force and with the use of high tech weaponry.) There is virtually no other version of power represented to children in the mass media and in the mass toy markets. The idea of power *with* others rather than power *over* others is not expressed. Other dimensions of heroism besides physical strength are absent. With this colonization of children's minds going on it is no wonder what peace has been a hard concept to sell to children. War is literally where the action is. Peace is not nearly as exciting—not as long as it is conceived of in static or passive terms, ie. as an absence of fighting. However, it is clear to me from talking with the children at Downtown Alternative School that their concrete experiences as Peace-makers has developed in them a much deeper understanding of peace—one that is active rather than passive. Non-violent living with others (resolving conflicts without physical force or verbal put-downs) is understood by the children to be very difficult and demanding work.

One little boy described the Peace-maker role in almost Supermanesque terms—"It's really exciting. You swoop in to where kids are fighting and help solve the fight." But while Peacemakers intervene actively, they do not take power away from participants (eg. by bossing them around) but rather exercise a new kind of power *with* them by collaboratively working through the conflict within the agreed-upon framework.

Peacemaking is not all glamour and excitement, though. As one little girl said: "When you first come up to them (the kids who are fighting) it's fun. Then it's not so fun—there is a lot of talking to do." The children identify peacemaking as strenuous both emotionally and mentally. The interplay of conceptual and emotional work is challenging. As children become capable of more abstract operations (around 6 or 7 years) they want to master things that are hard (not just simple stuff) and conflict resolution is not a game for those with faint hearts or weak knees. In fact one of the issues I was concerned about in talking to the children was whether the Peacemaker role was appealing to the boys as well as the girls. Some of the skills involved in peacemaking are more traditionally feminine and nurturant—eg. empathetic listening and naming feelings. But, the peacemaker role is actually an androgynous one, mixing skills from the male side of the spectrum as well. A good peacemaker has to be assertive in digging for the truth and in keeping people on track when a compromise is being negotiated. And there are cognitive skills involved that combine the analytic-deductive and the intuitive (figuring out people's underlying motives, sizing-up what compromise might satisfy both sides) and these seem to appeal to both boys and girls (much as detective games seem to cross sex boundaries in their appeal).

In interviewing the children, it was clear to me that they greatly admired their classmates who were good at peace-making and aspired to be like them. This was true even for the little boy in class who was most prone to physical aggression against other children. When I asked him what he thought would be hardest for him about being a peacemaker he said: "You have to do it without touching kids." He too identified with the role and wanted to learn to be a peacemaker. For me, this was the most convincing evidence that a clear alternative version of power and heroism was present for the children who had taken part in the peacemaker project.

For more information about the Peacemakers call Joey Noble at (416) 535-7258 or Anne Lacey (one of the teachers at Downtown Alternative School) at 393-1882. The children have worked out several dramatizations to show how the programme works and have already given several performances at schools and conferences. A group of children have also written a storybook on the theme of conflict resolution. Plans are under way to make a videotape that will try to capture the everyday process of conflict resolution in the classroom and on the playground.

RESOURCES

BOOK LIST

We have endeavoured to include titles that should be readily available at your local library or bookstore. Please note that in some cases the publisher will have sold rights outside of their own country. Therefore, the publisher source listed may not be correct in your region, but a bookstore or library can still source the book based on title and author information.

BOOKS FOR ADULTS

Educating for Global Responsibility, Betty A. Reardon, editor. Columbia Teacher's College Press, 1988.
A teacher-designed curriculum (K–12) for peace education. Includes detailed annotated biography and organization list, curriculum materials.

Comprehensive Peace Education: Educating for Global Responsibility, Betty A. Reardon. Columbia Teacher's College Press, 1988.
Theory and pedagogy.

Who's Calling the Shots: How to Respond Effectively to Children's Fascination with War and Play and War Toys, Nancy Carlsson-Paige and Diane E. Levin. Philadelphia: New Society Publishers, 1990.

The War-Play Dilemma: Balancing Needs and Values in Early Childhood Classrooms, Nancy Carlsson-Paige and Diane E. Levin. Philadelphia: New Society Publishers, 1990.

Helping Young Children Understand Peace, War and the Nuclear Threat, Nancy Carlsson-Paige and Diane E. Levin. National Association for the Education of Young Children, Washington, D.C. (Tel: 1-800-424-2460).

Peace Education, A Bibliography Focusing on Young Children, Rosemarie Greiner. Resource Centre for Nonviolence, 515 Broadway, Santa Cruz, CA. 95060 (Tel: 408-423-1626).

Interracial Books for Children Bulletin, Vol. 13, No. 6 & 7, 1982.
This is a special double issue bulletin devoted to issues of militarism

and education. Includes bibliography of books and audiovisual materials and several articles on working for peace. Available from: 1841 Broadway, New York, NY, USA 10023.

Learning the Skills of Peace Making, Naomi Drew. Jalmar, 1987. An activity guide for elementary-school children on communicating cooperating and resolving conflict.

A Manual on Nonviolence and Children, New Society Publishers, Philadelphia, 1984. A handbook for parents and teachers on creating a positive environment for children to learn cooperation and conflict resolution. Includes games, songs, book lists, advice on developing parent and child groups and on facilitating meetings.

The Peace Book, Bernard Berenson. Bantam Books, 1982. An illustrated story about world problems in terms children can understand. Useful for generating ideas about how to simplify complex information.

Peace-ing It Together, Pat Fellers. Winston, 1984. Classroom tested activities covering conflict resolution, world interdependence.

Talking to Children About Nuclear War, William and Mary Wicker Van Orum. Continuum, 1984. Practical advice on how to listen and respond to children's fears.

Watermelons Not War: A Support Book for Parenting in the Nuclear Age, New Society Publishers, Philadelphia, 1984. A book written by five mothers who provide basic information about nuclear weapons and nuclear power; suggestions for answering children's questions and how parents can help each other.

BOOKS FOR YOUNG PEOPLE

Preschoolers:

Nicholas, Where Have You Been? Leo Lionni. Knopf, 1987. Nicholas discovers that a species supposed to be an enemy can really be friendly.

The Butter Battle Book, Dr. Seuss. Random House, 1984.
A cold war situation escalates over the silly issue of which side of the
bread to butter. Typical Seuss, with a serious theme.

Grades Kindergarten to 3:

Potatoes, Potatoes, Anita Lobel. Bowmar/Noble Publishers, 1967.
A mother tries to prevent her two sons from going to war.

The Hating Book, Charlotte Zolotow. Harper & Row, 1969.
The problem of fighting with your best friend.

The Pig War, Betty Baker. Harper & Row, 1969.
An I CAN READ history book about the rivalry between two groups,
each of whom thinks an island belongs to them.

Planting Seeds, Patricia Quinlan. Annick Press, Toronto, 1989.
A young girl, after watching a TV show about nuclear bombs,
questions why people build them. Her parents offer sound advice
which encourages her to think more deeply about the subject.

Beast, Susan Meddaugh. Houghton Mifflin, 1981.
Her family said the beast was strong and ferocious, but Anna was the
only one who really knew anything about the beast.

Drummer Hoff, Barbara Emberly. Prentice-Hall, N.J., 1967.
A rhyming story about an army preparing for battle.

The Fight, Ginette Anfousse. Heritage/Editions la courte echelle,
1978.
A little girl's fight with a boy down the street gives her a black eye and
the understanding that fighting is no fun at all.

The Story of Ferdinand, Monro Leaf. Viking Press, 1938.
Classic story of the bull who didn't want to fight.

The Stranger, Kjell Ringi. Random House, 1968.
Townspeople bring out a cannon to protect themselves from a giant
who turns out to be friendly.

Grades 4 to 6:

The Weaver's Horse, Jill Creighton. Annick Press, 1990.
Set in the Crusades, this story addresses the question of the individual's response to the brutality of war and the quest for peace.

War Boy: A Country Childhood, Michael Foreman. Arcade; McClelland & Stewart, 1991.
Foreman also illustrated this collection of vignettes from his childhood during World War Two.

Park's Quest, Katherine Paterson. Lodestar/Dutton; Penguin, 1989.
A young boy searches for information about his father, who was killed in the Vietnam war.

Naomi's Road, Joy Kogawa. Oxford University Press, 1986.
Little Naomi and her older brother are sent by themselves to an internment camp for Japanese Canadians during WWII.

Number the Stars, Lois Lowry. Houghton Mifflin, 1989.
A ten-year-old Danish girl helps rescue a Jewish family from the Nazis during WWII.

The Little Weaver of Thai-Yen Village, Trán-Khán-Tuyét. Children's Book Press, San Francisco, 1987.
A true and sensitive story of a young Vietnamese orphan who is brought to the U.S. Text is in English and Vietnamese.

A Child in Prison Camp, Shizuye Takashima. Montreal, Tundra Books, 1971.
Memories of childhood in a WWII prison camp for Japanese Canadians.

Hockeybat Harris, Geoffrey Bilson. Kids Can Press, Toronto 1984.
After living through the bombing of London during World War II young David is shipped off to Canada to live with strangers.

My Shalom, My Peace, Jacob Zim, editor. McGraw-Hill; Sabra Books, N.Y., 1975.
Paintings and poems about peace by Arab and Jewish children.

Sadako and the Thousand Paper Cranes, Eleanor Coerr. Dell
Yearling, 1977.
A fictionalized account of a Japanese child-heroine, Sadako, who had
leukaemia from the bombing of Hiroshima.

The War Party, William O. Steele. Harcourt Brace Jovanovich, 1978
(A *Let Me Read* Book.).
A young Native American looks forward to his first battle, but is
horrified by the experience.

Angel Square, Brian Doyle. Toronto, Groundwood Books, 1987.
Grades 4 and up.
Tommy takes his life in his hands as he attempts the daily crossing of
Angel Square, where children of different religious backgrounds battle
it out every day. The trick is to have a friend from each group!

The Dog Who Stopped the War, Betty Waterton. Toronto,
Groundwood Books, 1985. Grades 4 and up.
Christmas vacation begins with a war between two armies of kids,
complete with snow-fort, helmets, shields and lots of snowballs. But it
takes the death of a dog for the kids to make peace.

In a Big Ugly House Far From Here, Magda Zaglan. Toronto, Press
Porcepic, 1982. Grades 4 and up.
A collection of stories about a Hungarian girl during WWII.

The Last War, Martyn Godfrey. Collier Macmillan, 1986. Grade 4
and up.
In Montreal after a nuclear blast, two boys live by their wits.

Lisa, Carol Matas. Toronto, Key Porter 1987. Grade 4 and up.
Danish teenagers organize to fight the Nazi invasion during WWII.

Thirteen Never Changes, Budge Wilson. Scholastic-TAB, 1989.
Grades 4 and up.
Living in Halifax at the time of World War II, a thirteen-year-old girl
romanticizes war. But gradually, and often painfully, she learns about
the value of peace.

Peace Begins With You, Katherine Scholes. Little, Brown and Co.,
1989. Grade 4 and up.
Using picture-book format, poetic musings on the many meanings of
peace.

Grade 5 and up:

Alan and Naomi, Myron Levoy. Harper & Row, 1977.
A powerful portrait of Naomi, who is sent to live with her American relatives after being traumatized by her experiences in France during WWII.

Conrad's War, Andrew Davies. Crown, 1980.
A bizarre story of a young boy's fantasies about war, killing and guns.

The House of Sixty Fathers, Meindert DeJong. Harper Trophy, 1956.
A young boy makes his way alone through enemy territory after the Japanese invade China.

The Game on Thatcher Island, T. Degans. Viking, 1977.
Harry is flattered when a group of older boys invite him to participate in their game of war on Thatcher Island, but his elation disappears when the game takes a terrifying turn.

The Big Book for Peace, Ed. Ann Durrell and Marilyn Sachs. Dutton Books, 1990.
A collection of stories about war and peace by popular children's writers like Lloyd Alexander and Natalie Babbit.

How the Children Stopped the War, Jan Wahl. Avon Books, 1976.
Children as peacemakers. Illustrated.

The Machine Gunners, Donald Westall. McKay/Greenwillow, 1976.
British children during WWII assemble a machine gun out of scavenged parts and decide to secretly participate in the war.

Martin Luther King, Nigel Hunter. Wayland, 1985.
A short biography of the civil rights leader who believed that "non-violent protest was the way forward for Black Americans."

Grade 6 and up:

The Boy's War: Confederate and Union Soldiers Talk about the Civil War, Jim Murphy. Clarion; Houghton Mifflen, 1990.
Uses letters and diaries to look at experiences of boys under the age of 16 who fought in the American Civil War.

Five Days of the Ghost, William Bell. Stoddart, 1989.
A young Canadian boy in China witnesses the events at Tienanmen Square.

Fireweed, Jill Paton Walsh. Macmillan (UK), 1969.
Two runaways in the confusion of the London blitz try to find peace and security, but reality cannot be escaped for long.

Ghandi, Kathryn Spink. Hamish Hamilton, 1984.
A short biography of the great Indian political leader and social reformer who believed in passive resistance.

Grade 7 and up:

The Cripples' Club, William Bell. Stoddart, 1988.
George is a Southeast Asian refugee who has blocked out the horrors of his past. Only when he makes friends does he slowly gain the courage to face his war-time experiences.

The Root Cellar, Janet Lunn. Penguin, 1983.
Rose Larkin travels back to the time of the American Civil War, where she learns that war is not a very pretty experience.

Promises to Come, Jim Heneghan. Overlea Press, 1988.
Becky resents Kim, the Vietnamese teenager who is adopted into her family, while Kim is haunted by painful memories.

Peace and War, Ed. Michael Harrison and Christopher Stuart-Clark. Oxford University Press, 1989.
An international anthology of poems about war and peace.

In Search of Peace: Winners of the Nobel Peace Prize, 1901–1975, Edith Patterson Meyer. Abingdon, 1978.
About the Nobel Peace Prize and its recipients with an emphasis on individual efforts to keep humanity cooperating and at peace.

FILMS AND VIDEOCASSETTES

The Hoarder, Director: Evelyn Lambart, 1969, 7 min. 35 sec.
National Film Board of Canada. K – Grade 6.
A greedy blue jay takes whatever he can from others. Not even the
sun's rays are safe from his greed. When everything becomes grey and
lifeless, he realizes the error of his ways.
Issues: economics, insecurity, greed, conflict, cooperation.

The Big Snit, Director: Richard Condie, 1985, 9 min., 49 sec.
National Film Board of Canada. Grade 3 and up.
An animated film about two simultaneous conflicts—the microcosm of
a domestic quarrel and the macrocosm of a nuclear holocaust—and
how each is resolved.
Issues: conflict resolution.

Bombs Away, 1988, 17 min. 2 sec. National Film Board of Canada.
Grade 4 – 8.
A 12 year old girl has nightmares that she is the only person left after a
nuclear war. She feels she cannot talk to anyone about her fears and
refuses to join the peace movement. She eventually finds a way to
conquer her fears and becomes more optimistic about the future.
Issues: war fears, empowerment, conflict resolution.

Top Priority, Director: Ishu Patel, 1981, 9 min. 9 sec. National Film
Board of Canada. Grade 4 – Adult.
Animation film in which a family in an unspecified Third World
country are left in desperation when, instead of a water pump and
irrigation pipes, a long-awaited convoy brings the military and missiles
for a border war.
Issues: violence, the relation of militarism to Third World poverty,
economics, the individual and authority.

"E", Director: Bretislav Pojar, with Francine Desbiens, 1981, 6 min.
32 sec. National Film Board of Canada. Grade 5 – Adult.
An "E" is usually an "E" but occasionally someone might see it as a
"B." What follows depends on who is doing the seeing. An ordinary
citizen may end up in a prison cell or psychiatric ward, or even have to
undergo a lobotomy to "correct" the vision. A person who happens to
be a ruler, however, can control how other people see things.
Issues: media, perceptions, social attitudes.

The Day Off, Director: Sidney Goldsmith, 1980, 10 min. 10 sec.
National Film Board of Canada. Grade 10 – Adult.
In this animated film people relaxing on a beach are constantly being
reminded of tragic events happening elsewhere.
Issues: media, individual choice, despair, passivity, activism.

Prelude to War, Film (tape version available), Simon Wiesenthal
Holocaust Center. Distributed by Facing History and Ourselves. Grade
10 – Adult.
Prelude to War was one of seven films in the Why We Fight series
made by Frank Capra. These movies were used for orientation of U.S.
soldiers to explain the reasons for WWII. The films were so effective
that they were commercially released. This is an excellent film to use
in discussions of propaganda.
Issues: media, war.

Consuming Hunger, USA, 1988, 3 parts 30 min. each, video, colour.
DEC Films (Canada), Maryknoll Society Center (USA).
Television and the famine in Africa. Television, which links millions of
people in the developing world, has become the principal instrument
we use to respond to Ethiopia. *Consuming Hunger* examines how
television shapes our understanding of global issues.
Issues: media, economics, Third World.

Eye of the Storm, videotape, 27 min. colour, Social Studies School
Service. Distributed by Facing History and Ourselves. Grade 7 –
Adult.
In 1970, Jane Elliott, a third grade teacher in a small Iowa town,
divided her class into two groups for a lesson in discrimination—one
group being superior to the other. While only a classroom experiment,
the experience had a profound and lasting effect on the students.
Issues: racism, prejudice.

*Eyes on the Prize II: America and the Racial Crossroads 1965–1985,
Part IV, The Promised Land (1967–1968),* videotape, 54 min.
Distributed by PBS Enterprises. Grade 7 – Adult.
Illustrates connections between the war in Vietnam and the problem of
poverty in the United States and analyzes the nonviolent protest
movement led by Martin Luther King.
Issues: economics, racism, nonviolence, civil rights.

Neighbours, Director: Norman McLaren, 1952, 8 min. 10 sec.
National Film Board of Canada. Grade 6 – Adult.
This classic film-without-words is a parable about two people who
come to blows over the possession of a single flower.
Issues: the roots of violence, war and militarism, conflict resolution,
choices, attitudes and values.

A Day at School in Moscow, U.S./Soviet Union, 1987, 24 min. colour,
video. DEC Films (Canada), Center for Psychological Studies (USA),
Grade 7 – Adult.
A Day at School in Moscow takes you inside the front door of a
Moscow school. It shows kids ranging in age from six to sixteen and
compares Soviet and North American schooling.
Issues: stereotypes, education.

Children of War, Director: Premika Ratnam, 1986, 25 min. 20 sec.
National Film Board of Canada. Grade 7 – Adult.
A documentary in which teenagers from war-torn countries tell
Canadian high-school students about the struggles in their homelands
(El Salvador, Guatemala, Northern Ireland, Namibia, East Timor and
Zimbabwe).
Issues: the realities of war, oppression, international relations,
economics, racism, media, human rights.

In a Box, Director: Elliott Noyes Jr., 1967, 4 min. 2 sec. National
Film Board of Canada. Grade 7 – Adult.
A clever line-drawn illustration of how our perceptions restrict and
'box' us in and how, in the face of anything unfamiliar, we tend to rush
back to the security of the boxes we know, no matter how restrictive
they are.
Issues: perceptions and attitudes, self-deception.

Mile Zero—The Sage Tour, Director: Bonnie Sherr Klein, 45 min.
National Film Board of Canada. Grade 7 – Adult.
A documentary about four Montreal high school students who took a
year off school to talk to their peers about the importance of preventing
nuclear war. "The Peace Kids" spoke to over 120,000 young people in
150 communities.
Issues: war, media, politicians, teachers, youth.

Faces of the Enemy, videotape, 57 min., colour. Social Studies School Service. Distributed by Facing History and Ourselves. Grade 7 – Adult.
Faces of the Enemy is a fascinating look at how the media uses visual images to shape our ideas of the enemy.
Issues: media

Hell to Pay: Bolivia and the International Monetary Fund, England/ Bolivia, 57 min. video, colour. Distributed in Canada by DEC Films. Distributed in USA by Women Make Movies. Grade 10 – Adult.
Bolivia should be a rich country, but it's not. Working women of Bolivia take viewers on a tour of their country and translate the statistics into reality.
Issues: Third World, economics.

Speaking Our Peace, Bonnie Sher Klein and Terri Nash, 55 min. video. National Film Board of Canada. Grade 9 – Adult.
Women in the Soviet Union, Britain, Canada and the United States talk about why they work for peace.

Film Distributor's List

Bullfrog Films
(specializes in children's material and distributes many Canadian films)
7 regional distribution centers in USA
Tel: 1-800-543-FROG

Canadian Filmmakers Distribution Centre
67A Portland Street
Toronto, ON M5V 2M6 Canada
Tel: (416) 593-1808

Canadian Filmmakers Distribution West
1131 Howe Street
Vancouver, B.C. V6Z 2L7 Canada
Tel: (604) 684-3014

Center for Psychological Studies in the Nuclear Age
1493 Cambridge St.
Cambridge, MA. 02139 USA
Tel: (617) 497-1553

DEC Film and Video
394 Euclid Ave.
Toronto, ON M6G 2S9 Canada
Tel: (416) 925-9338

Facing History and Ourselves
25 Kennard Rd.
Brookline, MA 02146 USA
Tel: (617) 232-1595

Learning Corporation of America
Coronet Films
108 Wilmot Rd.
Deerfield, IL 60015 USA
Tel: (708) 940-1260

Maryknoll Society Center
Maryknoll, N.Y. 01545 USA
Tel: (914) 941-7590

MPI Home Video
15825 Rob Roy Drive
Oak Forest, IL. 60452 USA
Tel: (708) 687-7881

National Film Board of Canada (NFB)
(7 regional offices in Canada)

National Film Board of Canada (USA)
1251 Avenue of the Americas, 16th floor
New York, N.Y. 10020 USA
Tel: (212) 586-5131

Public Broadcasting System Enterprises (PBS)
13220 Braddock Place
Alexandria, VA. 22314 USA
Tel: (703) 739-5400

Pyramid Films
P.O. Box 1048
Santa Monica, CA 90406 USA
Tel: (213) 828-7577

Simon Wiesenthal Holocaust Center
9760 West Pico Boulevard
Los Angeles, CA 90035 USA
Tel: (213) 553-9039

Social Studies School Service
P.O. Box 802, 10200 Jefferson Boulevard
Culver City, CA 90232 USA
Tel: (213) 839-2436

WEWS–Cleveland
1300 Euclid Avenue
Cleveland, OH 44115 USA
Tel: (216) 431-5555

Women Make Movies
225 Lafayette #212
New York, N.Y. 10012 USA
Tel: (212) 925-0606

CANADIAN ORGANIZATIONS AND JOURNALS

Canadian Peace Alliance (CPA)
555 Bloor Street West, Suite 5
Toronto, Ontario. M5S 1Y6 Canada
Tel: (416) 588-5555

A coalition of 300 Canadian peace groups. Publishes quarterly
magazine, Peace Report, and The Canadian Peace Directory, an
annotated 1988 guide to approximately 500 groups; helps member
groups to launch public education and political action campaigns;
maintains computerized listing of peace resources in Canada which
can help you locate a group, speaker, film, publication or resource
center in your region or subject area.

Canadian Peace Educator's Network
c/o Pembina Institute
P.O. Box 7558
Drayton Valley, Alberta. T0E 0M0 Canada
Tel: (403) 542-6272

Publishes directory of Canadian and international groups involved
with formal education on peace issues; "Dialogue" newsletter; runs

Canadian Environmental Project; provides lists of resources for teachers.

Educators for Nuclear Disarmament
Capilano College – 2055 Purcell Way
Vancouver, British Columbia. V7J 3H5 Canada
Tel: (604) 986-1911
Matthew Speier

(See Teaching Peace)

Project Ploughshares
Conrad Grebel College
Waterloo, Ontario. N2L 3G6 Canada
Tel: (519) 885-0220, fax: (519) 885-0014

A church-based umbrella organization specializing in research, publishing, and advocacy; produces and distributes books, videos, and pamphlets on peace for parents and children.

Canadian Voice of Women for Peace (VOW)
736 Bathurst Street
Toronto, Ontario. M5R 2R4 Canada
Tel: (416) 537-9343

VOW is a network with links to individuals and groups in other countries who are working for peace, justice, disarmament and a safer world environment. VOW is active in campaigning against war toys and games. Publishes a quarterly newsletter, have audio-visual materials available for loan, a library with books on women and peace, and a Speakers Bureau.

Pacijou Collective
c/o Diane Savird
3582 Rue Chambly
Montreal, Quebec. H1W 3J9 Canada
Tel: (514) 523-7266

A French Canadian organization working with children against war toys and games.

International Youth for Peace and Justice Tour

c/o David Fuchs
1435 City Councillors Rd.
Montreal, Quebec. H3A 2E4 Canada
Tel: (514) 842-5374

Once a year, this non-profit, educational organization brings an international group of young people to Canadian schools where they talk to students about their experiences of war and social conflict. The organization has an educational guide for teachers to provide their students with background on the countries from which the touring youth come.

Our Schools, Our Selves

1698 Gerrard Street East
Toronto, Ontario. M4L 2B2 Canada
George Martell

A magazine for Canadian education activists which provides a forum for discussion of progressive education and social justice issues. Covers a broad range of educational issues and practice. Also publishes books for education activists.

Teaching Peace

4540 W. 6th Avenue
Vancouver, British Columbia. V6R 1V5 Canada
Tel: (604) 986-1911, ext. 2459
Matthew Speier, Ed.

Teaching Peace is published twice a year by the Peace Education Centre and includes information, articles and analysis about children and war. The Centre also sponsors an annual Youth for Global Awareness Conference for secondary students.

AMERICAN ORGANIZATIONS AND JOURNALS

Peace Child Foundation

National Office
9502 Lee Highway
Fairfax, Virginia. 22031 USA
Tel: (703) 385-4494

A national organization with 20 local chapters which promotes international and inter-cultural understanding through creative programs in the arts. Kids are involved in specific programs in the United States and trips abroad are arranged. *Peace Child* also brings kids from other countries to the United States to participate in its conflict resolution and other peace-related programs. *Peace Child* publishes a newsletter four times a year, and can supply teachers with curriculum materials.

Children's Creative Response to Conflict (CCRC)
Box 271
Nyack, New York. 10960 USA
Tel: (914) 358-4601

Offers workshops for children in USA and abroad focusing on themes of cooperation, communication, affirmation and conflict resolution. Have published a handbook, *The Friendly Classroom for a small planet*, and a songbook, *Children's Songs for a Friendly Planet*. They also publish a tri-annual newsletter called Sharing Space, and have a variety of other materials available. Has affiliates all over the USA and in Canada.

Facing History and Ourselves
25 Kennard Road
Brookline, Massachusetts. 02146 USA
Tel: (617) 232-1595

Provides resource materials and workshops focusing on themes of democracy, totalitarianism (particularly in the context of World War Two) and examines issues like the abuse of power, obedience to authority and popular resistance. Uses history to help students consider how racism, anti-semitism and violence affect them now. The Facing History foundation provides training for teachers and other adults to design programs. They also publish books, an annotated bibliography on the Holocaust, and a newsletter.

Educators for Social Responsibility
23 Garden Street
Cambridge, Massachusetts. 02138 USA
Tel: (617) 492-1764

A professional association of educators who work with teachers to help students develop into socially responsible critical thinkers and decision-makers. ESR runs professional development workshops and conferences throughout the U.S. They publish and distribute educational materials and members receive a newsletter, special program reports, a discount on all ESR publications, and advance notice of all conferences and professional development opportunities.

Parenting for Peace and Justice
4144 Lindell #400
St Louis, Missouri. 63108 USA
Tel: (314) 533-4445
Jim or Kathy McGinnes

PPJN is an interfaith, interracial, transnational association which links families interested in peace and justice.

It shares ways families can affect social forces that threaten family/community/global well-being. It provides leadership training and workshops; resources include bi-monthly newsletter; books, teachers handbooks and videos.

Center on War and the Child
P.O. Box 487
Eureka Springs, Arkansas. 72632 USA
Tel: (501) 253-8900

This organization provides books, pamphlets, videos and educational resource packages for teachers and parents. The Center focuses on children as soldiers and as victims of war; with the socialization of children to accept violence (war games and toys). Members receive a quarterly newsletter.

Center for Psychological Studies in the Nuclear Age
1493 Cambridge St.
Cambridge, Massachusetts. 02139 USA
Tel: (617) 497-1553

A research institute which focuses on issues of international conflict, including the effect of violence on children. They have done research on environmental violence, violence in children's television, corporate decision-making and social change. They have produced books and videos on teaching children about non-violence and conflict-resolution. The Center has a resource list and will also send researchers to conduct seminars and workshops.

Center for Peace and Conflict Studies
Wayne State University
Detroit, Michigan. 48202 USA
Tel: (313) 577-3453

Provides booklets, bibliography, seminars on global conflict, human/children's rights.

The Lion and the Lamb Peace Arts Center
Bluffton College
Bluffton, Ohio. 45817 USA
Tel: (419) 358-8015 ext. 207

Promotes and studies peace through arts and literature for children.

Peace Resource Center
Pyle Center, Box 1183
Wilmington College
Wilmington, Ohio. 45177 USA
Tel: (513) 382-5338

Provides annotated catalogue of peace education resources available from the Center including books, audio-visual materials and curriculum materials dealing with global conflict and conflict resolution.

Rethinking Schools
1001 East Keefe Ave.
Milwaukee, Wisconsin. 53212 USA
Tel: (414) 964-9646
Michael Trokan—office manager

A quarterly journal with a national perspective focusing on elementary and secondary schools. The journal looks at classroom and social policy issues; promotes educational equity and progressive education; includes curriculum ideas.

Dr. Susan Goldberg is a Research Scientist at the Hospital for Sick Children in Toronto. Her special interest is the study of the development of parent-child relationships.

Dr. Goldberg grew up in New York City in a family of social activists. In 1982, when she was a well established researcher in the area of early social development, she realized that she could use her professional training and experience to make a unique contribution to the peace movement.

She began by undertaking research on children's awareness of the nuclear arms race. As she began to compile information, Dr. Goldberg began running workshops for parents, educators and community groups on how to talk to children about nuclear issues. These were conducted under the auspices of Parents for Peace, a group in which she was a central figure. The materials collected and produced for these workshops was published in 1985. From that time on, Dr. Goldberg has delivered talks and lectures about her research at international meetings.

When active war broke out in the Persian Gulf, Dr. Goldberg received daily requests from educators as well as the popular media to give advice about how to discuss current events with children. This, as well as her ongoing work with parents and educators, convinced her to compile *Times of War and Peace*.